BURT FRANKLIN: RESEARCH & SOURCE WORKS SERIES
Philosophy & Religious History Monographs 155

BOETHIUS

" .   .   . *My wordes here and every part*
I speke hem alle under correccioun."

BOETHIUS

AN ESSAY

HUGH FRASER STEWART

BURT FRANKLIN
NEW YORK

Published by LENOX HILL Pub. & Dist. Co. (Burt Franklin)
235 East 44th St., New York, N.Y. 10017
Reprinted: 1974
Printed in the U.S.A.

Burt Franklin: Research and Source Works Series
Philosophy and Religious History Monographs 155

Reprinted from the original edition in the University of Minnesota
    Library.

Library of Congress Cataloging in Publication Data

Stewart, Hugh Fraser, 1863-1948.
    Boethius: an essay.

    Reprint of the 1891 ed. published by W. Blackwood, London.
    Includes index.
    1. Boethius, d. 524.
B659.Z7S7 1974   180   74-20524
ISBN 0-8337-4935-8

Dedicated to

THE REV. JOHN EARLE, M.A.

RECTOR OF SWANSWICK,

AND

RAWLINSONIAN PROFESSOR OF ANGLO-SAXON IN THE
UNIVERSITY OF OXFORD,

AS AN UNWORTHY TOKEN OF

GRATITUDE AND ESTEEM.

PREFACE.

THE original essay, of which these pages are a development, won the Hulsean Prize at Cambridge in December 1888. My excuse for their appearing so long after the event, must be the rare leisure of a schoolmaster's life; my excuse for their appearing at all, lies in the conditions of the founder's will. The trustees of Dr Hulse's benefaction generously granted me, more than two years ago, permission to expand and improve my manuscript; but an essay of this kind can never be more than prodromic and tentative, and the subject is too wide to be adequately treated in a single volume of reasonable dimensions. Some of the chapters, notably those which deal with the influence of Boethius on medieval thought and literature, would furnish material each for a separate treatise.

With regard to the present work, I ought perhaps

to specify how and in what degree it differs from my original scheme. The part that remains intact is chaps. i., iii., and iv. Chaps. ii. and v. had to be rewritten—the one because I could no longer honestly say that I agreed with Dr Hodgkin's explanation of the 'Trial,' the other because I could no longer regard the 'Anecdoton Holderi' as conclusive evidence of the authenticity of the Tracts. Chap. vii. is entirely new, and will, I hope, fill up a gap in the argument. Chap. vi. has been altered beyond recognition. The pages of it which deal with 'Beowulf' may seem a little out of place in a chapter professedly confined to vernacular translation; but, to be honest, I could not refrain from airing my views on the sources of the strange philosophical element in that poem.

My warmest thanks are due to those friends who have helped me in my work,—to Professor Hort for reading chap. vii. in manuscript; to M. Paul Meyer for performing a like office for chap. vi., and offering many suggestions and some invaluable criticism; and above all to Professor Earle, who has crowned a long course of kindness by allowing this little book to go out with his name inscribed upon it.

MARLBOROUGH, *April* 1891.

CONTENTS.

BOETHIUS.

CHAPTER I.

A GLANCE AT THE CONTROVERSY ON BOETHIUS.

Authorities.—The volumes of Nitzsch and Hildebrand mentioned in this chapter have been of great assistance to me in following the course of what may be called the Boethian controversy.

HE who in our day would enter on a study of Boethius is confronted at the very threshold by the question, " Was the writer of the ' De Consolatione Philosophiæ ' a Christian ? " This, the first of all questions to which the modern student requires an answer, does not seem to have troubled the readers of the old Roman in the middle ages, on whom his influence was so real and so profound, much less the scholars of the Renaissance. For although it was to him, more than to any other, that Europe was indebted for an acquaintance with the higher flights of Hellenic thought, at a time when the original vehicle of its expression seemed lost beyond hope of recovery, yet men soon forgot the great teacher and translator in their delight at the new gift of a Greek literature, free to all the world.

A series of dogmatic tracts, a close intimacy with certain prominent Christians of his time, and a tragic death almost coincident with a threatened persecution, had all helped to invest Boethius with a halo of sanctity to which he had in reality but little claim. For more than a thousand years, from the eighth to the eighteenth century, he was generally accepted as the undoubted author of the tracts above mentioned, and as a martyr for the Faith into the bargain. Alcuin (735-804) has a word of praise for the treatise 'Quomodo Trinitas,' and there are traces of another treatise of Boethius in his book 'De Fide Trinitatis.' Paul the Deacon in the same century calls him *vir catholicus*,[1] and this title is emphasised not long afterwards by Ado,

[1] In Muratori rer. Italicar. scriptor., tom. i. p. i., Mediol., 1723, p. 103.

archbishop of Vienne,[1] who, in the 'Breviarium Chronicon,' distinctly states that Theodoric put Symmachus and Boethius to death *pro catholica pietate*. This tradition, whether it had its first origin in the words of Ado or only received a fresh impulse from them, would naturally bring the theological writings of the patriot-statesman into special prominence. By the thirteenth century it had taken so firm a root, that Vincent of Beauvais did not hesitate to refer their composition to an attack on his orthodoxy, which Boethius was bound to defend.[2]

There is a faint fore-note of the future debate to be heard in the commentary on the 'Consolation' ascribed to Bruno of Corvey (tenth century), where it is remarked that the spirit of this book is not exactly a Christian spirit,—that there are many thoughts in it that savour too much of Platonism, and are at variance with the teaching of the Church. But this early commentator, with a critical perception which allows him to join hands across the centuries with Baur and Hildebrand, was ready to admit that the writer's object was not to dispute the truths of Christianity, but only to open to the unlearned the sealed books of Greek philosophy.

[1] A.D. 800-875. [2] Spec. Hist., xxi. 15 ; xvii. 56.

John of Salisbury (1110-1180), on the other
hand, while he recognises to the full the charm and
value of the 'Consolation,' does not attempt to justify or explain the absence from it of the incarnate
Word.[1]

The question lay dormant for a long while, such
later commentators as Murmellius [2] and Grotius [3]
making no effort to reconcile the apparent discrepan-
cies existing in the different branches of Boethius's
work, till at the beginning of the last century Gott-
fried Arnold, with scant ceremony, deprived him of
all title to the authorship of the tracts, and dubbed
him simply pagan.[4]   The flame which this spark
kindled has burnt fiercely enough round the *Boethius-
frage* ever since—in Germany and France, at least;
and Hand went even further than Arnold had gone,
in denying to Boethius any outward connection with
Christianity at all.[5]   Twenty years later Obbarius
followed on the same side, defending this position at
greater length.[6]   In our own time the chief com-
batant of Boethius as a theologian has been F.
Nitzsch, who, while he denies the authenticity of the

[1] Policratic., lib. vii. cap. 15.
[2] See his commentary in Migne, lxiv. c. 1240.
[3] Proleg. ad Hist. Goth, &c.   Amsterdam, 1655.
[4] Unparteiische Kirchen- und Ketzerhistorie.   1700.
[5] Hallesche Encyklopädie von Ersch und Gruber.   1823.
[6] In his critical edition of the De Consolatione.   Jena, 1843.

tractates, admits the probability of at least an outward adherence to Christianity on the part of a
Roman statesman who held high office under a Christian government, was hailed as friend by a circle of
cultivated Christians, and, finally, was closely connected by marriage with a nobleman of conspicuous
piety.[1]

To this formidable list of German learning and
research must be added the names of Le Clerc,
Judicis de Mirandol, Du Roure, and Jourdain. Of
these four French writers, the only one that deserves
our particular attention here is M. Charles Jourdain,
who some thirty years ago endeavoured to cut the
knot of the question by the ingenious hypothesis
that the theological tractates attributed to the philosopher were the work of an African bishop of the
same name—not an uncommon one, it would seem,
in the sixth century—who was exiled to Sardinia
under the persecution of the Arian king Thrasamund,
suffered martyrdom there, but lost his identity in the
more conspicuous personage of his Roman namesake.[2]
But the indiscreet zeal of M. Jourdain led him into
the same error into which Hand and Obbarius had

---

[1] Das System des Boethius. Berlin, 1860.

[2] Mémoires présentées à l'Académie des Inscriptions et Belles
Lettres, tome vi. 1860.

fallen. He did not see that by cutting off Boethius
from all connection with Christianity, he put him
outside the pale of political life at Rome in the
reign of Theodoric—a heretic king, it is true, but one
who always upheld the tradition of his predecessors
from Theodosius onwards, that a profession of Christianity was the indispensable qualification for hold-
ing office, and who never repealed the stringent laws
against paganism laid down in 390.

The first writer who made any systematic attempt
to vindicate Boethius's Christianity was Glareanus.[1]
Unable to harmonise the philosophy of the ' Consolation ' with the theology of the tracts, he adopted
the simple if somewhat audacious expedient of ex-
alting the latter at the expense of the former.   In
other words, he challenged the authenticity of the
' Consolation.'   It is almost unnecessary to say that
this absurd supposition has not found favour with
modern critics. The equally extravagant theory started
by Gervaise, that in the person of Philosophy Boethius
allegorically concealed our Lord ; that the consolatory
apophthegms addressed by her to the pupil, " whom
she had nourished on all the learning of the Eleatic
and Academic schools," are the utterance of the
Word of God,—went no further than its author's

1 Preface to the Basle edition of 1546.

' Histoire de Boëce '[1] and died a speedy death. Happily for Boethius, his orthodoxy has found more trustworthy though perhaps less ingenious champions. We may not, indeed, cite as such Berti[2] or Francheville[3] or Richter[4] or Suttner[5] or Schündelen,[6] for they all considered the ' Consolation ' an unfinished work, and the five books which have come down to us as nothing more than the foil against which Boethius intended by-and-by to set the immeasurable superiority of the consolations afforded by the Christian religion. The upholders of this theory take their stand on certain *validiora remedia*, which Philosophy at the very outset of the dialogue promises that she will presently apply to her suffering disciple, and which they maintain she has not yet applied when the book breaks off. It is undoubtedly true that the work is two-thirds over before she sees fit to fulfil her promise, and exclaims " Sed quoniam te ad intelligendum promptissimum esse conspicio, crebras coacervabo rationes " ;[7] but from this point forward

1 Histoire de Boëce, sénateur romain.   Paris, 1715.
2 Preface to the Leyden edition of 1611.
3 Nouvelle Traduction.   A la Haye, 1744.
4 Translation of the Cons.   Leipzig, 1753.
5 Programm des Eichstätter Lyceums.   1852.
6 Theologisches Litteraturblatt.   Bonn, 1862, 1870, 1871 (different articles).
7 Cons., iv. pr. 2.   But see p. 61, and cp. Cons., ii. pr. 5.

her utterance continues to gain in vigour and authority : the subjects attacked are more difficult, and
consequently the arguments advanced are more elaborate, and demand a keener attention and a more
robust intelligence, than those of the earlier books ;
the bursts of song with which her tired listener was
wont to be refreshed are heard at rarer intervals, and
the prose passages are of longer breath.[1]

Besides, the arrangement of the dialogue, its
gradual growth from the merely rhetorical and
apologetic to the speculative, the way in which the
threads—and they are many and perplexed—are
gathered together in Philosophy's closing speech,
appear to me irresistible evidence of the completeness of the whole.

An interesting and very plausible explanation of
Boethius's position was offered by G. Baur in 1841.[2]
According to him, Boethius was both philosopher
and theologian, but philosopher first and theologian
afterwards, taking in this last capacity a curious
interest in subtle points of dogma, which he endeavoured to illustrate by the light of pagan learning.

---

[1] Even before this, in Bk. iv. pr. 6, she says : " quamquam angusto
limite temporis sæpti tamen aliquid deliberare conabimur,"—words
which show that Boethius had some suspicion how short his time
was, and that what he had to say must be said quickly.

[2] De Boethio Christianæ doctrinæ assertatore. Darmstadt, 1841.

Dr Hildebrand shows, in his recent work on Boethius and his Christianity, that he is of much the same way of thinking.[1] To be chronologically consistent, this book ought to be noticed with those written after 1877—*i.e.*, since the discovery of the 'Anecdoton Holderi'; but the author, as he tells us himself (*op. cit.*, p. 19, note 2), did not hear of the fragment in question until his investigation of the tracts was practically finished, and was led to believe in their authenticity on purely internal evidence. With regard to the 'Consolation,' he considers that Boethius meant it to be a sort of " apologia pro vita sua,"—a defence of his labours in the cause of philosophy. There is a great deal to be said for this view. But I think the learned doctor makes too much of the influence which Christianity had upon Boethius in writing his last work, and he seems sometimes a thought too subtle in his endeavours to read between the lines. R. Peiper, to whom we owe the first critical edition of the tracts,[2] does not go very deep into the controversy, and confines his choice, based upon MS. evidence, to the first three (see p. 109). It is not easy to see

[1] Boethius u. seine Stellung zum Christenthume. Regensburg, 1885.

[2] In the Teubner Text edition of the Consolation and Tracts. Leipzig, 1871.

why he refuses to include the fifth, which, as Usener remarks, has very nearly as good MS. right to be considered genuine as the others. There can be little doubt, however, that he is perfectly justified in rejecting the fourth, " De Fide," and not all Biraghi's ingenuity and keenness of sight [1] can convince us that this tract was not inserted before the book against Nestorius by some mistake. Of this more anon, when we come to examine the religious writings more closely.

The name of the venerable Girolamo Tiraboschi is entitled to more respect than his compatriot's ; but although there is much sound sense in his remarks on Boethius's influence on scholasticism, he does not offer us much assistance towards solving the question of his Christianity.[2] Puccinotti [3] and Bosizio [4] are two more Italians who appear between them to have written a good deal on our author, but I have not had the advantage of seeing their works.

[1] To which he lays claim in his Boezio, filosofo, teòlogo, martire a Calvenzano. Milan, 1865.

[2] Storia della Letteratura Italiana, tom. iii. parte i. Florence, 1806.

[3] Il Boezio, &c. Florence, 1864.

[4] (a) Memoria intorno al luogo del supplizio di Severino Boezio : Pavia, 1855 ; (b) Sul cattolicismo di A. M. T. S. Boezio : Pavia, 1867 ; (c) Sull' autenticità delle opere teologiche di A. M. T. S. Boezio : Pavia, 1869.

I have purposely reserved to the last the most important piece of external evidence we possess as to the authenticity of two at least of the tracts. This is the so-called 'Anecdoton Holderi,' a fragment found about 1877 by Alfred Holder[1] on the last page of 'Codex Augiensis,' No. cvi.[2]   This MS., which came, as its name implies, from the monastery at Reichenau (Augia Dives), and now reposes in the Grand-Ducal Library at Carlsruhe, is a tenth century copy of the 'Institutiones Humanarum Rerum' of Cassiodorus.   The fragment, however, with which we are concerned seems to have no connection with that educational treatise beyond a common authorship.

It consists of a title and dedication, and three paragraphs, — the first giving an account of the works and character of Symmachus, the second performing a like office for his son-in-law Boethius, and the third dwelling at somewhat greater length on the learning and dignities of Cassiodorus.

The paragraphs relating to Symmachus and Boethius are worth transcribing in full :—

"Symmachus patricius et consul ordinarius, vir

[1] Hermann Usener, in his exhaustive monograph on the subject— Bonn, 1877—speaks of the discovery as quite a recent one.

[2] The famous Codex Augiensis is of course the Græco-Latino uncial MS. of St Paul's Epistles, now in Trinity Library.

philosophus, qui antiqui Catonis fuit novellus imitator, sed virtutes veterum sanctissima religione transcendit. Dixit sententiam pro allecticiis in senatu, parentesque suos imitatus historiam quoque Romanam septem libris edidit.

" Boethius dignitatibus summis excelluit, utraque lingua peritissimus orator fuit. Qui regem Theodoricum in senatu pro consulatu filiorum luculenta oratione laudavit. Scripsit librum de sancta trinitate et capita quædam dogmatica et librum contra Nestorium. Condidit et carmen bucolicum. Sed in opere artis logicæ id est dialecticæ transferendo ac mathematicis disciplinis talis fuit ut antiquos auctores aut æquiperaret aut vinceret."

The original work, of which this tantalising excerpt is all that has come down to us, seems to have been a letter on the literary history of his own family, written by Cassiodorus about 522. There are two reasons for fixing on this date. The letter stands addressed to Rufius Petronius Nicomachus, Magister Officiorum. To this name Usener would add Cethegus, surmising that it was indistinctly written in the MS., and so was left out by the copyist. (It is surely more natural to suppose that it was passed over by inadvertence.) Now Rufius Petronius Nicomachus Cethegus is perfectly well

known as Consul in 504, and Master of the Offices
in 522, and this date corresponds exactly with the
consulship of Boethius's sons (522) mentioned a few
lines below it.

Dr Hodgkin appears to accept unquestioningly all
that Usener has to say on the 'Anecdoton,' and
speaks of our certain knowledge that Boethius wrote
the tracts.[1]   I am unable to regard the German
editor's conclusions as final.   His commentary on
the fragment is indeed a marvel of microscopical
investigation, but he is guilty of one glaring in-
consistency;[2] and the glib way in which he assigns
this sentence to the epitomatiser and that to Cassiodorus does not inspire confidence.   In a dis-
connected scrap of MS. like this, who shall draw the
line between copy and original?

It is laying too great a burden on the 'Anecdoton'
to claim for it that it puts the authenticity of the
tracts beyond the range of doubt.   The handwriting
is not earlier than the tenth century; the date of the
supposed original is partly based upon a conjecture,
however plausible; the Latin of it is too bad; the

[1] Italy and her Invaders, vol. iii. p. 566.
[2] In one breath he speaks of the title of the MS. as having been
tampered with (p. 8), and in the next he supports its genuineness
by the fact that Cassiodorus is not called " præfectus prætorio "
(p. 71)!

praises of Cassiodorus (" vir eruditissimus . . . dum laudes regis facundissime recitasset ") are too loudly sung for the words to be those of that writer himself. Still, no one will deny its great value as contributory evidence, and it remains a formidable weapon in the hands of the champions of Boethius's Christianity.

CHAPTER II.

BOETHIUS AND THEODORIC.

Authorities.—The 'Anonymus Valesii,' described in the text; the writings of our author himself, and especially the 'Consolation'; the 'Variæ Epistolæ' of Cassiodorus, which Dr Hodgkin has translated *en abrégé* (London, 1886), supplemented by the 'Anecdoton Holderi'; some of the letters of Ennodius, bishop of Pavia, and the same writer's 'Parænesis Didascalica.' For the general history of the period I have consulted Du Roure's 'Histoire de Théodoric le Grand' (Paris, 1846), Deltuf's 'Théodoric, Roi des Ostrogoths et d'Italie'; and of English historians, Gibbon in his 'Decline and Fall,' Milman in his 'History of Latin Christianity (1854), and Hodgkin in the second and third volumes of his 'Italy and her Invaders' (Oxford, 1880 and 1885).

THE fall of the western portion of the empire which Constantine had founded dates in reality from the death of Valentinian in 455. That prince, the last of the house of Theodosius, had, by his vacillating policy and extravagant taxation, driven crowds of his subjects into voluntary exile, and cleared the

way for the hordes that hovered over the entry of
every road that led to Rome, and that swooped down
on the defenceless city like vultures on a wounded
tiger. The history of the latter part of the fifth
and of the beginning of the sixth century is the
history of the rivalry between Huns and Vandals,
Visigoths and Ostrogoths, for the prize of Italy.

From the inhabitants themselves, the degenerate
descendants of the Fabii and Metelli, there was little
resistance to be feared. The old Roman spirit was
dead, and the feeble senate was powerless to stem
the torrent of barbarian conquest. The successors
of Valentinian in the palace of the Cæsars disappear
at the rate of one in every two years, and this in
itself is sufficient witness to the violence of the
changes that shook that proud fabric, and to the
rottenness of the political and social life of the
age.

It was reserved for Odovacar, the rough young
soldier whose high destiny was foretold by Saint
Severinus,[1] to administer the *coup de grâce* to the
stricken empire. We know nothing certain about
his origin beyond the fact that he was the son of one
Edecon, identified by Gibbon, but with great improb-
ability, with the Edica who was left on the bloody

[1] See the story in Hodgkin, *op. cit.*, vol. ii. p. 527.

field of Bollia, where the power of the Scyri was once and for ever broken.[1] After a life of wandering amid the wild tribes of Noricum, the young barbarian found his way to Italy at a time when it was filled with a soldiery envious of the good fortune of their brethren in Spain, in Gaul, and in Africa, and clamouring for their share of the spoil,—for a third part of town and vineyard and field. Orestes the patrician, who, although he had for sufficient reasons refused the purple in favour of his son Augustulus, was still the real sovereign of the West, resisted such an outrageous demand. This resistance was Odovacar's opportunity. Putting himself at the head of the disaffected troops, he stormed and sacked Pavia, and caused Orestes, who had fled thither at the first alarm, to be put to death. The wretched Augustulus, whom he deemed unworthy of his vengeance, he was content to sentence to a luxurious exile in the Lucullan villa.[2] He had now only to stretch out his hand to grasp the imperial sceptre, but experience had taught him that this was a dangerous bauble. He accordingly addressed a letter through the Roman senate to the emperor Zeno at

[1] For an exhaustive discussion on the parentage of Odovacar, see Hodgkin, *op. cit.*, vol. ii. pp. 528-530.

[2] On the bay of Naples, the famous seat of Lucius Lucullus, the conqueror of Mithridates.

Constantinople, in which he formally advocated the abolition of the Western empire, and begged to be invested with the title and rank of patrician. The prospect of an undivided rule from Byzantium to Britain flattered Zeno, and he readily gave his assent.

Odovacar kept strictly to the letter of his proposal, and although after seven years he revived the consulship of the West, he never showed any inclination to fill the office in person, but confided it to trustworthy Roman officers. From 476 to 490 he ruled the land with justice and tolerance, protecting it by his arms from the active aggressions of barbarians on the frontier, and by his prudent administration from the still more dangerous oppression of his own turbulent soldiery. But Odovacar's successful course was now to be crossed by one of the most romantic and pathetic figures in all history. This is not the place to dwell at length on the early life of Theodoric the Ostrogoth, but a brief sketch of it is necessary to a right comprehension of the causes that led to the passage of the Isonzo, where Italy once again changed masters. The son of Theudemir the Amal and Erelieva his wife,[1] he was born in 454,

---

[1] She is generally spoken of as his concubine. Dr Hodgkin (*op. cit.*, vol. iii. p. 15) inclines to the view that the union between her and the Amal was sanctioned by the Church, although the woman was of inferior rank to the man.

on the very day of the Ostrogothic victory over the Huns. At the age of eight he exchanged the rough roving life of his father's camp for the comfort and ease of the royal court at Constantinople, where he remained for ten years as a hostage for the alliance which the emperor had entered into with the barbarians. It cannot be said that the young Amal profited greatly by the careful education bestowed on him, for, if we are to believe the statement of the 'Anonymus Valesii,' he could to the last only sign his name through a stencil. When his father died in 474, Theodoric succeeded to the hereditary leadership of the Ostrogoths, and soon gave evidence that his hand was better fitted to the sword than the style. He appears to have been an active agent in the restoration of Zeno when he was driven into exile by the usurper Basiliscus; and the various military enterprises in which he was engaged between the years 477 and 488, now for the emperor against his revolted generals, now for his own hand against his patron, gave him a wide experience. So that when the cautious Zeno tried to check the growing power of his young ally by pitting against him his namesake Theodoric Strabo (the squint-eye), an unscrupulous adventurer, who, jealous of his rival's superior birth and influence, was for ever scheming to supplant him in the favour of the Gothic people, he found that the hostage of Constantinople, the nursling of the court, had, like the lion-cub of Æschylus, become too formidable to be trifled with. Accordingly, he was only too glad to fall in with the Amal's suggestion that he should pass over to Italy and win her from Odovacar to the Roman empire once again. Towards the end of 488 Theodoric left Wallachia at the head of an enormous multitude—we have no certain knowledge of its exact number, but the lowest computation puts it at forty thousand fighting men, with their wives and families, amounting in all to something like two hundred thousand souls.

The march went on all through the winter of that year, and the spring and early summer of the following, amid dangers and difficulties the magnitude of which it is not easy to measure. For besides the anxiety of providing provisions for a whole nation, there was the active resistance of the wild tribes to be reckoned upon, through whose territory the road to Italy lay. Notwithstanding a great and signal victory over the Gepidæ, who barred the passage of the Ulca, innumerable other conflicts with the same Gepidæ or with the Sarmatians kept Theodoric and his host on the farther side of the Alps until August 489, when he at last descended into Italy, to find

Odovacar confronting him on the banks of the Isonzo. Step by step the stubborn king was driven back, from the Isonzo to Verona, from Verona to Ravenna, where he held out for three years till hunger and despair forced him to capitulate. A treaty was arranged by John, archbishop of Ravenna, and it seemed as if Odovacar was to reap in Theodoric's clemency the reward of his own forbearance towards Augustulus fourteen years before. Not only were his life and safety assured to him, but it was agreed upon oath that the rule of Italy should be equally divided between conqueror and conquered. A week's holiday of friendship and parleying was crowned by a banquet held to celebrate the union of the rival kings. Odovacar came in all confidence, in answer to Theodoric's invitation, and was in the act of receiving the petition of two suppliants, who held him by the hand in the earnestness of their appeal, when a couple of soldiers placed in ambush in the hall rushed forth to slay him. " But when they saw him," writes the chronicler,[1] " they were afraid, and would not set on him." Upon this Theodoric ran up, and with a brutal jest and rough reply to Odovacar's helpless call on God—ποῦ ὁ Θεός ;—cleft

[1] Johannes Antiochanus, in Karl Muller's Fragmenta Historicorum Græcorum (Paris, Didot, 1841-72), tome v. p. 214a.

him from chin to loin.   Nor did the furious Ostrogoth rest content with one victim.   Odovacar's
brother was shot down as he fled through the palace
garden ; his wife Sunigalda was starved to death in
prison ; and their son Ocla was sent as a hostage to
Gaul, whence he presently escaped only to meet a
bloody death at the hands of his father's murderer.

Thus did Theodoric seal in blood his charter of
conquest.   But when once his vengeance was
glutted, when once he had received the emperor's
consent to his mastership of Italy, he devoted himself heart and soul to the carrying out of Odovacar's
prudent plan of government.   For thirty-three years
the realm enjoyed peace and prosperity ;—peace, for
Theodoric, as often as his northern frontier was
threatened by Gaul or German, moved his court
from Ravenna to Verona[1] or Pavia, whence he
could easily check any barbarian advance ; prosperity, for he was sagacious enough to see that it
was to the real interest of Italy that Goths and
Italians should be rigidly kept apart, the former
receiving the long wished for *tertiarum distributio*,
as a reward for past services, and as an inducement

---

[1] Theodoric's connection with Verona survives in the name " Diet-
rich of Bern," under which he figures in the old High-German
romances of the middle ages.

to protect the rights of the natives; while these last were encouraged to cultivate without let or hindrance the rich resources of the land, which revived wonderfully during these quiet times. He thus restored to Italy something of her ancient splendour and supremacy, and the ambassadors who crowded to Ravenna from every country in Europe went away filled with wonder at the wisdom of the king and the magnificence of his court.[1]

It was during this last expiring flicker of Roman glory that Anicius Manlius Severinus Boethius [2] moved across the scene; and his is one of the names that reflects lustre on the reign of Theodoric, while it lays the stigma of undying shame on the memory of the senate which pronounced his most unmerited condemnation, and of the king who had it carried out.

We cannot be certain of the exact year of his birth, but it most probably fell somewhere this side of 480 A.D.[3] His father, Aurelius Manlius Boe-

[1] Cf. Decline and Fall, c. 39 ; and Var., 6, 9 ; 7, 5.

[2] Boethius, and not Boetius, is the way the name should be written. See Usener, Anec. Hold., p. 43.

[3] The limits of the date of his birth are 475 in the one direction and 483 in the other. We know that he died in 524, and just before his death we hear him speaking of the signs of premature decay, of the old age of sorrow, that he bears upon his body—

" Intempestivi funduntur vertice cani
    Et tremit effeto corpore laxa cutis."—Cons. i. m. 1.

Now grey hairs cannot be called untimely at the age of fifty. He

thius, was the trusted servant of Odovacar, and under that monarch filled successively the posts of præfectus urbi (this he held twice), præfectus prætorianus, and consul (in 487). He dying while his son was still a boy, the education of the young Anicius was intrusted to friends of high standing in the state. These friends were, according to tradition, none other than his own kinsmen, Festus and Symmachus, the latter of whom further testified his affection for his ward by bestowing on him the hand of his daughter Rusticiana. The tradition that Boethius was first married to one Helpes, daughter to Festus (was the name of his other guardian chosen for the sake of symmetry ?), has long been given up. It rested solely on the insecure foundation of a supposititious tombstone at Pavia, which bore witness to the virtues and wifely devotion of a Sicilian lady who was led to Rome by love for her lord, whose name, be it remarked, does not appear in the epitaph at all.

It will not, I think, be stretching conjecture too far to assume that Boethius's first acquaintance

must have been born after 475. Besides, Ennodius, born about 473, writes of him and to him in quite a fatherly way (Paraenesis Didiscalica, Migne, 63, c. 254 ; Letters, Book vii. No. 13), which he could hardly have done to a man who was only a few years his junior. On the other hand, neither could his sons, who were elected consuls in 522, have been much less than twenty, nor their father less than forty at the time. He was therefore born before 483.

with Theodoric dated from the year 504, when, as a
lad of twenty, he must have seen that celebrated
entry into Rome, when the heretic conqueror was
welcomed to the city of St Peter by the shouts of
the people and the reverence of priests and Pope.
A youth so distinguished by birth, fortune, and ac-
complishments would naturally command the early
notice of the Amal, whose presence at Rome just
then was in great measure due to his wish to win
the favour of the leading men there, and who would
be only too glad of the chance thus offered him of
ingratiating himself with them by a ready recognition of the powers and promise of their rising
generation. Besides, it is easy to imagine the charm
which such a personality would exercise on the barbarian king, who could appreciate in others the
culture that had been bestowed upon himself in
vain. For Boethius, though young in years, was
already old in learning. A born student, he chose
to pass his hours of leisure with his books rather
than in the spectacles and amusements, the battles
of the Blues and Greens, that engrossed the Roman
youth. The diligence with which he devoted himself to the pursuit of knowledge was rewarded by
an unusual versatility and an encyclopædic erudition. No branch of science or art remained long

neglected or unattempted by him; and, thanks to
the liberal training of his guardian, he enjoyed the
rare privilege of being able to read the Greek philosophers in their own tongue.[1]

As Horace made it his chief boast

> " Princeps Æolium carmen ad Italos
> Deduxisse modos,"

so it was the literary object and aim of Boethius to
import Greek wisdom into his native land. To this
end he translated the works of Pythagoras on music,
of Ptolemy on astronomy, of Nicomachus on arithmetic, of Euclid on geometry, of Archimedes on
mechanics. Finally, he sought to bring the whole of
Greek speculative science within the range of Roman
readers ; and though he did not live to see the attain-
ment of his ambition, he managed to give to the
world in something less than twenty years, of which
several were absorbed in the discharge of public
duties, more than thirty books of commentary on,
and translation of, Aristotle. These embraced
nearly all the logical works of the Stagyrite—

---

[1] See Cassiodorus, Var., i. 45. There is not the smallest foundation
for the tradition that he was educated at Athens. Cassiodorus distinctly says, " Atheniensium scholas longe positus [not *positas*] in-
troiisti." The undoubtedly spurious 'De Disciplina Scholarium' is
the only one of the works attributed to Boethius that breathes a word
on the subject, and such an exceptional training would have been
sure to receive mention, either by himself or by one of his friends.

the 'Topica' and the 'Analytica,' the 'Categoriæ' and the 'De Syllogismo'—and they further make good their author's title to the inheritance of the Academy in the West, and mark him as the pioneer of the scholastic philosophy. But Boethius did not confine his pen within the limits, however wide, of pagan learning. He rushed, with more ardour perhaps than discretion, into the lists of theological controversy, and endeavoured—not to identify the old philosophy with Christianity, as some of the new Platonists were inclined to do, but—to apply its methods to the treatment of doctrinal difficulties.

The favour of the king and the traditions of his own family—the Anicii had been distinguished in the public service for the last six hundred years— combined to bring him into early contact with great affairs. At the age of thirty he was introduced into the senate with the title of patrician, an honour usually reserved for faithful and tried servants on their retirement from public life ; and the year 510 saw him elected sole consul. Undoubted as his qualifications both of character and intellect were for a high position of trust, it must be a source of unceasing regret that he felt himself bound to give practical illustration to Plato's theory that the happiest states are those which are governed by philosophers,[1] that he ever brought himself to exchange the seclusion of his own library for the turmoil of the Senate House. Within those walls, shining with glass and ivory, on which he had lavished all the adornment that taste could suggest or money could buy, he would have found a rest which the dusty struggle for office and distinction could never give, and his beloved books would have proved more faithful friends to him than the cowardly colleagues who condemned him without a hearing to disgrace and death. Happily he had leisure even in the busy time of his consulship to continue his literary and mechanical work, and we find him called away from his ordinary duties, now to construct a water-clock for Theodoric's brother-inlaw, Gundobad, king of the Burgundians, now to select a harper for the court of Clovis the Frank, now to help convict the guards' paymaster of an attempt to cheat the men with light coin. Higher still and higher he rose in the esteem and confidence of the king, till in the year 522 the cup of his pride was filled by the elevation of his two boys, Symmachus and Boethius, to the dignity of the consulship. On this occasion he was chosen to pronounce the customary panegyric on his royal

[1] Rep., vi. 487.

master, who showed his appreciation of the zeal and
loyalty of the panegyrist by appointing him *magister
officiorum*—a post which involved constant attendance
on the king's person, and which, as he tells us, had
never before been bestowed on a *privatus*.

But all the honours heaped upon him only serve
to heighten the tragedy of his sudden fall.   A burst
of ill-timed enthusiasm for the ancient Roman liberty
aroused the slumbering suspicion of the Ostrogoth,
who soon showed that he could hate as well as he
had loved ; while the servile and nerveless senate was
easily induced to hand over without a murmur the
noblest of its number to his vindictive vengeance.

The circumstances of his arraignment and condemnation are important enough to claim a closer
attention, and involve a scrutiny of one of the
most interesting, as it certainly is one of the most
perplexing, state-trials on record.   Moreover, the
very truthfulness and common honesty of Boethius,
apart from any question of political wisdom, are
here at stake, and so I must crave the reader's
indulgence while I endeavour to cast upon the case
the different lights afforded by the ' Anonymus
Valesii,' by Procopius in his ' Gothic War,' by Boethius himself in the ' Consolation of Philosophy,' and
by Cassiodorus in his ' Miscellaneous Letters.'

The authorship of the fragment which takes its title from its discoverer, Henri de Valois, the seventeenth century scholar, and is to be found appended to the history of Ammianus Marcellinus, may in all probability be ascribed to Maximian, bishop of Ravenna from 546 to 556.

After a description of Theodoric's decrees for the protection of the Ravennese Jews, whose synagogue had been destroyed by the Christians, there follows this account of the trial of the senators:

"From this time the devil found occasion to subvert the man [Theodoric], who had been hitherto governing the state well and blamelessly. For he presently ordered that the oratory and altar of St Stephen, by the fountains in the suburb of the city of Verona, should be thrown down. He also commanded that no Roman should carry arms—no, not so much as a knife.

"Also, a poor woman of the Gothic nation lying under a porch, not far from the palace of Ravenna, brought forth four dragons; two of which were seen by the people borne along in the clouds from the west to the east, and cast into the sea; two were carried off, having one head between them. A star with a torch, which is called a comet, did appear, shining brightly for fifteen days, and earthquakes happened frequently.

"After this the king began suddenly to chafe against the Romans whenever he found occasion. Cyprian, who was then Referendary,[1] and afterwards Count of the Sacred Largesses, impelled by greed, laid an information against Albinus the patrician, on the ground that he had sent letters to the emperor Justin, which were hostile to the king's rule.

"As he was denying this before the court" ("revocitus dum negaret"), "Boethius the patrician, who was Master of the Offices, said to the king's face: ' False is the information of Cyprian; but if Albinus did it, then both I and the whole senate did it with one consent. It is altogether false, O lord, my king!' Then Cyprian with hesitation brought forward false witnesses, not only against Albinus, but also against Boethius, his defender. But the king was laying a snare for the Romans, and seeking how he might destroy them: he put more trust in the false witnesses than in the senators. Then Albinus and Boethius were taken in custody to the

---

[1] The *referendarius* held a post in the royal court of appeal, to which we have no corresponding term in our legal system. His duties appear to have included the casting into an intelligible form the claims of either side in a lawsuit.

baptistery of the church. But the king sent for
Eusebius, prefect of the city of Ticinum, and without
giving Boethius a hearing, passed sentence upon
him. The king sent and caused him to be put to
death on the Calventian property,[1] where he was
held in custody. He was tortured for a very long
time with a cord bound round his forehead, so that
his eyes started; then at last in the midst of his
torments he was killed with a club."

Two more short quotations from the ' Anonymus,'
and the reader will be in possession of the whole
story of Theodoric's vengeance,—of that pitiful exhi-
bition of barbarian fury which mars the last page of
a record, else one of the fairest in the history of
Italy. In the first we have the epilogue of the
tragedy, the death of Symmachus.

" Meanwhile Symmachus, the head of the senate,
was brought from Rome to Ravenna. The king,
fearing lest grief for his son-in-law should lead him
to attempt something against his rule, had him accused and killed."

The second, which narrates Pope John's ill-fated
mission to Constantinople, is necessary to my present
purpose only in so far as it throws light on the later
tradition which numbered Boethius among "the

---

[1] The modern Calvenzano, in the province of Milan.

noble army of martyrs." This tradition was based upon a confusion of dates. The persecution of the Catholics, threatened but never carried out by Theodoric, is not heard of until after the execution of Boethius. The cause of this unkind promise is to be found in the proclamation against the Arians which the emperor Justin issued in the year 524. Behind the religious zeal which was the ostensible motive of this measure, it is easy to trace a wish to wean the Italians from their allegiance to the Ostrogoth. Theodoric felt this, and was no doubt indignant, and not unnaturally, that the studied toleration of his long reign should be so ungratefully requited by his eastern colleague.[1] And so he prepared to retaliate, and despatched the reluctant Pope John to Constantinople to make known his intention to the court there, and to demand from Justin that all heretics who had been compelled against their will to conform to Catholicism should be allowed to return to their own particular forms of heterodoxy.[2]

Despite his protestations, the unfortunate John was hurried on board ship, together with five other bishops, and in due course arrived at Constantinople.

[1] For the relations between the King of Italy and the Cæsar of Constantinople consult Hodgkin, *op. cit.*, vol. iii. chap. x.

[2] This seems to be the meaning of " ut reconciliatos hæreticos in Catholica restituat religione."

"And Justin the emperor," we are told, "came out to meet him as he had been the blessed Peter himself, and after giving him audience promised that he would do all else that was required of him, but that he could not by any means suffer the restoration to the Arian faith of those who had given themselves over to the Catholic religion. So when Pope John came back from Justin, Theodoric took him by craft, and laid the ban of his displeasure upon him.[1] After a few days John died." [2]

Writing less than a generation after the event, with the words of the imprisoned philosopher ringing in his ears, and hatred of the persecuting Ostrogoth rankling in his heart, Maximian would naturally be inclined to side with Boethius. Besides, a certain propensity for the marvellous and impossible should make us careful how we accept his account of things as strictly accurate. But in recounting the story of Boethius, there was little scope for the lively imagination that shows itself in the wonderful birth of the dragons, and the signs in the heavens that went before Theodoric's fit of frenzy. And

---

[1] "Et in offensa sua eum esse jubet."

[2] I have ventured, for the sake of clearness, to present these two last excerpts from the 'Anonymus' separately, although in the original the death of Symmachus is mentioned incidentally in the course of the narrative of Pope John's mission.

evidence so nearly contemporary, and so strikingly
coincident with Boethius's own version of the matter,
is entitled to the fullest measure of consideration.

It will be seen that Procopius, the Byzantian his-
torian (500-565 ?), bears out the words of the
'Anonymus.' "Symmachus and Boethius, his son-
in-law," he tells us in the first chapter of the first
book of his 'Gothic War,' "both of noble birth, were
chiefs of the Roman senate, and became consuls.
Their pre-eminence above their fellows in the practice of philosophy, their zeal for justice, the assistance they offered with their wealth to the poverty
of many, strangers and fellow-citizens alike, the
great renown they acquired,—all this combined to
stir up the hatred of villanous men. And when
they laid false information Theodoric believed them,
and slew the two men, on the charge of plotting
a revolution, and confiscated all their property."
Let us now hear what Boethius himself has to
say on the subject.[1]   After enumerating his various
services in the cause of his countrymen against
the oppression of greedy Gothic officials,[2] he under-

[1] Cons., i. pr. 4.

[2] Of special interest is his defence of the companions against an
edict of coemption (a fiscal measure which allowed the State to buy
provisions for the army at something under market price), which
threatened to ruin the province.   Hodgkin, by a comparison of this

takes to justify his defence of the senate's dignity and privileges which has brought about his present undeserved disgrace. " To save Albinus the consular[1] from the punishment consequent on a prejudiced trial, I braved the hatred of the informer Cyprian. It might well be thought that in so doing I incurred animosity enough, and indeed the very fact that my love of justice had left me no place of safety with the court-party ought to have rendered me more secure with the others. Now, who were the informers who struck me down ? Basilius, whom pressure of debt—he was long since expelled the king's service—drove to denounce me. Opilio and Gaudentius, who, on account of their countless and various crimes, had been ordered into exile by a royal decree. When they would not obey and sought sanctuary, and the king discovered it, he proclaimed that unless they had left Ravenna by a given day, they should be driven out with the brand of shame on their brows. Could any measure be more stringent ? And yet on that self-same day they laid information against me, and their information was admitted.

passage with certain letters of Cassiodorus (Var., iii. 20, 21, and 27), describing the disgrace of one Faustus, prætorian prefect, indentifies him with the governor whom Boethius dared to oppose. See *op. cit.*, vol. iii. p. 533.

[1] A member of the Decian gens—Consul in 493.

"Had my services merited this reward, thinkest thou? Or did the previous condemnation of those men invest them with a right to accuse? Had Fortune, then, no shame, if not for the innocency of the accused, at least for the infamy of the accuser? But thou wouldst know the heads of the charge under which I am arraigned. They say that I have desired the safety of the senate. How desired it? They accuse me of having prevented an informer from producing documents which were to prove the senate guilty of treason. What sayest thou, O my teacher? Shall I deny the charge for fear of putting thee to shame? But I did desire it, and shall never cease to desire it. Shall I plead guilty? Farewell, then, to the task of confuting the informer. Shall I call it a crime to have desired the safety of that illustrious order? It is true that by the decrees it issued against me it did its best to make it a crime. But stupidity, defeating as ever its own objects, cannot alter the rights of things, and, following the teaching of Socrates, I do not deem it right either to hide the truth or to confess a false-hood. Be this as it may, I leave the question to be weighed by thy judgment, and that of the wise. Still, in order that posterity may not miss the connection and the truth of the matter, I have com-

mitted an account of it to writing. As to those
forged letters by which I am accused of having
hoped for Roman freedom, what need is there to
speak of them ? Their forgery would have been
patent had I been allowed to make use of the
confession of the informers themselves,—a form of
evidence which in all cases carries the greatest
possible weight. (Indeed, what freedom is there
left us to hope for ? Would there were any !) I
would have answered in the words of Cassius, who,
when he was cited by Gaius Cæsar, the son of
Germanicus,[1] on the charge of being privy to a
conspiracy against him, replied, ' Had I known it,
thou shouldst never have known it.' Nor in this
affair has grief so dulled my sense as to make me
complain that wicked men have tried to outrage
virtue ; but I am exceedingly astonished that their
hopes have been crowned with success. For to
desire that which is evil is perhaps in the nature of
our mortal weakness, but that every rogue should
have power to carry out his designs against innocence is, under God's surveyance, monstrous.
Hence not without reason did one of thine own
disciples question — ' If God indeed is, whence
cometh evil ; and whence cometh good, if He is

[1] *I.e.*, Caligula.

not ? '[1]   But let us grant that it was natural that
evil-minded men, who were thirsting for the blood
of all good citizens, and of the whole senate, should
have sought my destruction, in whom they saw the
champion of both citizens and senate.   Did I
deserve the same treatment from the senators ?
Thou dost remember, as I think, since thou wast
ever with me to direct all my words and actions—
thou dost remember, I repeat, that day at Verona
when the king, thirsting for our general destruction,
sought to extend the charge of treason lodged against
Albinus to the senate as a body, and with what
indifference to my own safety I upheld the honour
of the whole order.   Thou knowest that these my
words are true, and that I have never boasted where
my own merit was concerned.   For a man lessens
in a measure the inward joy of a self-approving
conscience as often as he makes a parade of what
he has done, and is paid for it with fame.   Thou
seest clearly what has been the result of my integrity.   In place of the reward of real virtue, I am
undergoing the penalty of fictitious guilt; and was
there ever a confessed criminal who found his judges
so unanimous that some of them did not give way,
either from a knowledge of the frailty of mortal

[1] Epicurus, in the De Ira Divina, cap. xiii.

nature, or from a consideration of the circumstances
that wait on Fortune, to which all men alike are
liable? If I were charged with having attempted
to fire the temple of God, to slay His ministers with
sacrilegious sword, to compass the death of the good
and honourable,—even then sentence should have
been pronounced on me in my presence, and not
until I had confessed or been convicted. As it is,
all on account of an excess of zeal for the senate,
I have been condemned to death and loss of rights,
unheard and undefended, while nearly five hundred
miles away. Truly, its members deserve that no
one could ever be convicted on a like charge![1]
Those who brought the accusation knew well what
it was worth; and so, to darken it with the admix-
ture of some real crime, they lyingly asserted that
ambition for advancement had led me to stain my
conscience with sacrilege. But thou, who hast thy
dwelling ever within me, didst drive far from my
bosom's throne all desire for earthly things, and
sacrilege could not find a place before thine eyes.
Day by day thou didst instil into my ears and into
my meditation the saying of Pythagoras, ' Follow

[1] "O meritos, de simili crimine neminem posse convinci!"—*i.e.*,
they deserve, for their pusillanimity on this occasion, that no one
should ever be found to brave a tyrant's anger in defending their
rights.

God.' Was it likely that I, whom thou wast forming to perfection, to the very likeness of God, should seek the assistance of the foulest and vilest spirits? Besides, my unsullied hearth and home, the honoured friends who frequented it, my wife's father, a man without reproach and winning esteem by deed as well as name,[1] are my champions against all suspicion of such a charge."

And so he goes on, complaining to his divine consoler that they have besmirched her own robe in thus attacking the most devoted of her disciples, while he inveighs loudly against the unkind Fortune that suffers the innocent to be punished and lets the guilty go free.

Against this impassioned apology it is only fair to set the indirect evidence of Cassiodorus on the other side. The 'Variæ Epistolæ' of this writer are a collection of despatches concerning the administration of the kingdom, composed at the command and in the name of Theodoric and his successors. The bulk of them are addressed to Italian and Gothic officials; and overcharged as they are with laborious erudition and rhetorical adornment—to repeat his

---

[1] I retain the MS. reading, "æque actu ipso reverendus," and regard the expression as equivalent to "suis ipsius actibus reverendus." Cf. Obbarius's note on the passage.

barbarian master's orders in the simple and straightforward form in which they were doubtless issued
would have been impossible to the garrulous and
conceited old Italian—they afford us a most in-
structive insight into the scheme by which Theodoric sought to govern the land he had won with
his sword.

We know something of the career of Cyprian
from two of these letters ('Variæ,' v. 40, 41), and
we may form a fair conception of the man from the
hints they contain. The first of them announces
to Cyprian his elevation to the *comitiva sacrarum
largitionum*, the most important financial post in
the kingdom; the second recommends the newly
appointed officer to the notice of the senate.

Cyprian, we are told, was the son of one Opilio,
who held office under the unfortunate Odovacar.
The father had nothing to leave behind him but an
honourable name, but the young man soon began to
make his way in the world, thanks to his own
ability and the early favour of Theodoric, with
whom his duties as Referendary [1] brought him into
close and frequent communication. He seems to
have been gifted with a wonderful power of placing
the two sides of any question clearly and rapidly

[1] See above, p. 31, note.

before the court, and to have been able to state a complicated case just as well in the open air, as he rode by the king's side, as in the dry legal atmosphere of the council chamber.

The practical training, so much more valuable than any amount of theory, in which he had been schooled, stood him in good stead when he was despatched on an important diplomatic mission to Constantinople, and the imperial presence had no terrors for one who was familiar with the awful majesty of the Ostrogoth.

" Nihil tibi post nos potuit esse mirabile," Theodoric is made to say by his secretary, dead to all sense of humour. The envoy's knowledge of three languages, and his natural nimbleness of mind, enabled him to cope successfully with even the slippery Greeks.

What the precise object of this mission was we have no means of knowing, but we may guess that it was the occasion on which the intrigue between the senate and the emperor was discovered which brought about the trial at Verona.

The letter goes on to say that Theodoric has, in accordance with his usual procedure, thoroughly proved and tried the man whom he has chosen to honour, and that he has not found him wanting in any respect. Above all, Cyprian possesses faith, that most excellent gift, the bond of friendship between man and man, the pledge of reverent obedience to God. He is invited to enter upon the duties of Count of the Sacred Largesses, at the third Indiction (524-5),[1] and exhorted so to bear his honours in that office that the king may advance him yet higher.

The words of the document before us, together with those of a similar letter to Cyprian's brother, Opilio, which I shall notice next, make up a seemingly honourable record of public service. But a close consideration of it, and a comparison with the statements of Procopius, of the 'Anonymus,' and of Boethius himself, will, I think, enable us to see that the two accounts are not absolutely irreconcilable, and that the qualities which won Theodoric's admiration and Cassiodorus's concurrence are not such as would exclude the lower motives attributed to the informers by what may be called the counsel for the defence. Here we have a clever young lawyer, prac-

[1] The Indiction was an ever-recurring cycle of fifteen years, instituted, or, to speak more accurately, formally adopted by Constantine in 312. One such cycle began in September 522, and so the third Indiction from this date will be 524-5. For full explanation of the history of the system, and the method of computing it, see Hodgkin's Cassiodorus, p. 125, and "H. B." in Dict. Christian Ant., s. v. "Indiction."

tically a self-made man, whose chief claim to distinction lies in his ready wit and mental agility,
thanks to which he can state a case with such absolute impartiality as often to satisfy either of the
contending parties,—" alternæ parti indiscreta laude
placuisti." At the risk of appearing paradoxical, I
would say that scrupulous fairness of this sort is by
no means incompatible with a certain strain of un-
scrupulousness, and that a man who could deliberately
shut his eyes to the superior rights of one side or
the other in a lawsuit, need not necessarily have
been blind to his own interests. I do not for one
moment mean so far to lose sight of the difference
between the intellectual and the moral power as to
suggest that the one implies the other. I would only
remind the reader that success in the law, as in every
other profession, has sometimes been known to de-
pend on the energy with which a man can push his
own advancement, and the coolness with which he
can regard the claims of others. It is easy to imagine that Cyprian would look with envying eyes on
the honours heaped upon Boethius, and that he would
not be sorry for an opportunity of taking from him
his share in the king's affections and adding it to his
own. And now with Boethius's voluntary cham-
pionship of the accused senator came an unexpected

chance. The hesitation (there is no question of re-luctance, as Dr Hodgkin would seem to imply[1]) with which the 'Anonymus' tells us he extended his indictment to Boethius, may be accounted for by the flutter which the sudden appearance of that pattern of loyalty as the protector of treason would cause in the court, and further by a not unnatural doubt as to how the king would take an attack upon his Master of the Offices.

The event shows that his hesitation was baseless. Treason was abroad, and Theodoric meant to stamp it out, putting sternly aside all claims of friendship or of former services. And thus we see that as Boethius fell, involving in his ruin his father-in-law, Symmachus, and all his family, so Cyprian rose, carrying with him into the sunshine of royal favour Opilio, his brother, and Basilius, his connection, the former of whom shortly[2] received that same office of *comes sacrarum largitionum* which had become in a manner hereditary in his family.

Cassiodorus, who retained his post of quæstor, with its attendant duties of secretary and pamph-leteer, under Athalaric, the boyish successor of Theo-doric, writes in the warmest terms about the merits

[1] "With regret, but of necessity, Cyprian enlarges his charge." —*Op. cit.*, vol. iii. p. 545.
[2] In 527.

of a man whom we have lately heard Boethius denounce as a condemned felon. The letter, addressed
to Opilio (' Var.,' viii. 16), is particularly interesting,
as it appears to contain a covert allusion to the trial
of Boethius.

"You are to enjoy," the king writes, "all the
privileges and emoluments which were allowed to
your predecessors. Heaven grant that those who
stand firm in the strength of right action be not
shaken by any machinations of calumny. Time
was when even judges were harassed by informers.
But do you put away fear, you with whom is no
fault. Enjoy the fruits of your office. We lay on
you the same honours that adorned your brother;
do you imitate his faithful service. For in following him, you take honourable precedence of many.
He was a man whose opinion was highly respected,
whose steadfastness was proved. Under our great
forerunner he bore himself blameless, and adminis-
tered justice to the admiration of all." (Why, then,
that sentence about the machinations of calumny,
we are entitled to ask?) "It is easy to gauge the
value of his services, for under a successor who
had not known him, the whole court could not
abstain from singing his praises."

In the companion letter of recommendation to the

senate (' Var.,' viii. 17), the friendly rivalry of the two
brothers is held up to admiration.   With characteristic tautology, Cassiodorus assures his readers that
while the one preserves constancy in his friendships,
the other makes a point of fulfilling his promises
(" Amicitiis ille præstat fidem; sed magnam pro-
missis debet iste constantiam "); that the one is free
from avarice, and the other a notorious stranger to
covetousness.   Both have been faithful servants of
the king and trusted friends of their colleagues.
Opilio's manner of life (*victus*) has found favour with
the Goths, and his judicial decisions have satisfied
the Romans.   Indeed the fact of his having been so
often chosen arbiter in private suits is sufficient
testimony to the esteem in which his integrity is
generally held.

An honourable alliance with the house of Basilius
is also touched on.   Here we have a possible allusion to that Basilius who was " long since expelled
the king's service " (*vide supra*, p. 36).   The name,
indeed, appears to have been a not uncommon one
at the time; but all the actors in this drama are
so closely connected with one another, that we may
with the greatest probability assume the identification.   It may be mentioned here that in the ' Variæ,'
iv. 22, 23, the case is discussed of two senators—

Basilius and Prætextatus—who are charged with practising magical arts. They were handed over for trial to a board, on which Symmachus served with four others; and at this point we lose sight of them, for there is nothing to show how the trial went. One thing, however, is certain—that disgrace and withdrawal from public life would, in the existing state of the law, immediately have followed on a sentence of guilty. In our absolute ignorance of the issue, it would be dangerous to insist too strongly on the coincidence; but at least it is not without the bounds of possibility that this trial for magic gives us the key to Boethius's objection to his informer Basilius, " olim regio ministerio depulsus." Dr Hodgkin lays great stress on these letters of Cassiodorus, so flattering to the memory of the brothers Cyprian and Opilio; and he is inclined to attribute Boethius's passionate invective to the jaundiced mind of a student-statesman who, utterly unable to look upon things from any point of view but his own, would, when his vanity was affronted, sacrifice the cause of truth and the credit of his colleagues without a scruple. That Boethius was a man of harsh and hasty judgment, impatient of ignorance or dulness, unable to brook opposition in any form, I am prepared to admit. For instance, he calls his colleague

Decoratus, with whom he had been associated in some public office, "a wretched buffoon and informer"—"nequissimus scurra delatorque" (Cons., iii. pr. 4); what is more, he puts the unkind words into the mouth of his heavenly mistress. Now the only Decoratus we hear of at this date was a young man of great promise as an advocate, who had risen to be quæstor, winning in that capacity Theodoric's highest esteem and confidence. The king sought to honour his memory, for he died young, by advancing his brother Honoratus to the office he had left vacant. (We may be sure that Cassiodorus, who is here again our informant, will not let slip the opportunity of inserting a sententious remark about unconscious prophecy when he lights on two such significant names.) These official encomiums are always to be received with a certain reserve, but in this instance it would seem that the praise was not unmerited. A letter of Ennodius (iv. 27) testifies to the value set upon the young man's friendship by that worthy but wearisome bishop of Pavia.

But I do not see that we are justified, knowing what we do of the character of Boethius—of his high aims as a philosopher and a statesman, of his unshaken relations with Symmachus, the flower of integrity and uprightness—in imputing to him such a gross and inexcusable misstatement of fact, to call it by its mildest name, as we are bound to do, if we believe Opilio's past career to have been spotless. It must be remembered that Cassiodorus is writing merely as the mouthpiece of a barbarian monarch, and that the letters of his Miscellany, for all their wealth of " wise saws and modern instances," do not carry much conviction with them on questions of moral character.

And if Theodoric, who, barbarian though he was, had an intimate knowledge of human nature, could be led away by the plausible representations of clever informers into an act of blind cruelty, such as the condemnation of Boethius and Symmachus undoubtedly was, it is not unnatural that his well-meaning but not very discerning secretary should have fallen into the same mistake, and have recommended to Amalsuntha, the daughter of Theodoric and mother of the young Amal, those men who had won her father's approbation, as worthy to hold high office in the state.

The rigid silence, barring these hints in the letter to Opilio, which he guards on the question of the trial, and which Dr Hodgkin interprets as unfavourable to the king's decision, does not, to my mind, indicate anything more than an unquestioning adherence to his royal master's verdict, which as a true servant he must regard as irrefragable.

Gibbon's extraordinary statement that "the characters of the two *delatores*, Basilius and Opilio, are illustrated not much to their honour in the epistles of Cassiodorus," [1] is not borne out by the facts. The quaestor, speaking for the king, does unhesitatingly hold them up to the admiration of his countrymen; but *malo cum Platone errare*, and I for one would rather have to condone an error of judgment or an easily explicable piece of time-serving in Cassiodorus, than be driven to brand Boethius a liar with his last breath.

Whatever view we may take of the trial of Boethius, whatever value we may place on his apology, it must be freely acknowledged that failure was the end of his career as a practical statesman. The teller of the story of his life has no words with which to close it other than those with which he began it—a real regret, that must be shared by all who even at this distance of time have learnt to know and admire "the last of the Romans," that he should ever have chosen to forsake the life of contemplation for which he was so excellently fitted, for

[1] *Op. cit.*, chap. xxxix. *n.* 95.

one of action in times when tact was more necessary
to success than truthfulness, and at a court where
the breath of suspicion was so quickly fanned into
the desolating blast of hatred. And his was not that
barren contemplation where the thought is of the
inferior quality which finds its proper expression in
action, but that kind which Wordsworth praised as
producing works " which, both from their independence in their origin upon accident, their nature, their
duration, and the wide spread of their influence, are
entitled rightly to take place of the noblest and most
beneficent deeds of heroes, statesmen, legislators, or
warriors." For an insight into the man's personal
character, with its excellent qualities of devotion to
wife and children, of loyalty to his friends, and
unselfish zeal in the cause of the oppressed, we are
indebted to the letters of Cassiodorus and Ennodius
and his own great work. But we may search the
pages of the ' Consolation ' in vain for the Christian
virtues of humility and long-suffering. He reproves
himself through the mouth of his divine consoler for
petulance and impatience : the hints he lets fall in
the course of this book and elsewhere lead us to
suppose that he was fully aware of his intellectual
superiority over his contemporaries. It is doubtless
true that every honest and sincere worker always

knows the relative value of his powers, and of the results produced by them. A self-consciousness of this kind is not in itself in any way repugnant to the spirit of Christianity; it is nothing but the grateful acknowledgment of God's loan of talents. It is also true that the vaunted modesty of great minds, from Socrates downward, is too often assumed, and the merest affectation. But the total want of sympathy with the ignorance of the mass of mankind which our author everywhere betrays, is essentially opposed to the teaching of Him who thanked God that He had revealed unto babes the things that He had hid from the wise and prudent.

CHAPTER III.

THE 'CONSOLATION OF PHILOSOPHY.'

Rudolph Peiper has published a handy text with variants, &c., in the 'Biblioteca Teubneriana.' Leipzic, 1871. The vol. of Migne containing the 'De Cons.' is lxiii.

IT is a relief to turn from these gloomy details of suffering and death to the famous work for which we are indebted to that short year of prison life. My excuse for disregarding the probable chronological order, and taking the 'Consolation of Philosophy' before the religious tracts, lies in the obvious connection of that book with the sad story with which we have been occupied, in its indisputable authenticity, and in the larger insight it affords us into the character and mental attitude of the writer. For while, for reasons that shall presently appear, I cannot bring myself to see in the 'Consolation' Boe-

thius's confession of faith, or a tacit rejection of
Christianity; while I look upon both it and the
dogmatic chapters rather in the light of *prolusiones*,
though of very different scope, and composed under
very different circumstances,—yet it has for us the
higher value in that it contains a fairly systematic,
and in some measure original, scheme of philosophy.
The recollection of earlier studies and modes of
thought is so palpable in the various themes of the
' Consolation,' that the book may well stand as the
summary of Boethius's metaphysic; and there are
gleams of spontaneity amid its general artificial
constraint, which are noticeably absent from the
other writings of the great Roman translator.   Thus
the most important as well as the most grateful
duty of the student of Boethius is to make himself
early acquainted with this, his author's most characteristic utterance.   To this end I purpose giving
a short analysis of the five books: I shall then
proceed to examine the philosophical system it
encloses, endeavouring to show how far it was
borrowed from existing systems, and to what extent
it was influenced by that religion in which its
founder was born and bred.

Book I.

As Boethius lay in prison, longing for death to come and set him free from the misery of premature old age, and beguiling the weary hours with verse-writing, the favourite accomplishment of his happier days,[1] a mysterious visitor stood suddenly before his tear-dimmed eyes.   It is a woman, whose gleaming glance and bright complexion are in strange contrast with the years her generally venerable appearance proclaims, a form belonging to a bygone time. Her stature is beyond description wonderful, for now she raises her head to knock against the sky, and now she shrinks to the common measure of men.   She is clothed in a robe of her own weaving, whose gossamer web has stood the wear of ages, though there are rents in it that tell of rough usage at the hands of ignorant men.   On the lower hem is woven a π, on the upper a θ,[2] and they are connected by a series of lines arranged like the steps of a ladder.   In her right hand is a book, in her left a sceptre.   The sight of the Muses who are

---

[1] It is tantalising to read in the Anecdoton Holderi of a Carmen Bucolicum by the same hand that penned the De Consolatione.

[2] Standing for θεωρητική and πρακτική.   Boethius himself renders these two words by *speculativa* and *activa* respectively, in the first dialogue on the Isagoge of Porphyry.

waiting and weeping at the prisoner's bedside rouses her wrath, and she chases them away with words of contumely. Such sirens as they are not the fitting consolers of one who has been brought up under the shadow of the Porch and the Academy. She substitutes for their enervating elegies a sublimer strain of her own, gently reproving her hearer for his gloom and depression, and promising to cure him of his sickness. But first he must recognise who she is, and pronounce her name. Boethius gazes at her, but a strange lethargy binds his tongue, and it is not until she has wiped away his tears with gentle hand that he knows her for his beloved mistress Philosophy, the nurse of his early years and his oldest friend. He marvels at her deigning to leave her serene habitation in order to visit a poor prisoner; but she assures him that she has never yet abandoned those who truly love her. Anaxagoras and Zeno and Plato all enjoyed the consolation of her presence in their distress. But the physician must know the full extent of the patient's wound, ere she can lay on him her healing touch; and so she listens attentively to his story of the injustice and the wrong that have brought him to his present pass. The memory of his woes inspires Boethius; he cries aloud on God, the ruler

of the spheres, to declare why, when all things go
their round unswerving and unchanged, man alone
wanders at will, working wickedness; why the innocent lie helpless at the mercy of blind Fortune. His
divine visitor hears him out, and then compassionates
him on his banishment, or rather his self-imposed
exile, from his true home. She has been aware of
his wound long since, but it is deeper than she had
supposed. Her remedies must be cautiously applied,
and in increasing power, as the strength of the
patient grows. He shall lay bare his inmost heart
to her, and confess that indeed he knows not what
he is, nor what man himself is. There is One
above who rules and orders all things; but the
manner of this ordering is beyond the ken of the
sufferer's weakened intellect. Here, however, is
a spark of good from which a bright flame may
presently leap up. But it will need time.

Book II.

Philosophy now proceeds to prove that in reality
Boethius has no right to blame Fortune. He has
taken upon him, fully aware of what he was doing,
the yoke of her fickleness, whose very essence is
mutability. All the possessions the loss of which

he is now lamenting are Fortune's own property, and she can withdraw them at will. She had showered upon him the blessings of friends, riches, knowledge, and renown. Had any one of her votaries received more at her hands? To these arguments he answers with the words which Dante borrowed and made immortal [1]—" Of all the miseries of Fortune, the cruellest misfortune is to have been happy once." Philosophy replies that there are remaining to him blessings as precious as those he has lost. The noble Symmachus still lives, unscathed save by the pain another's sufferings are causing him. Rusticiana is left, and so are the young consulars, in whom their father and grandfather live again. How few there are who would not gladly change with even his present sad condition. True happiness lies within the man himself, and not in the gifts of Fortune, whose nature is so changeful, whose value is so variable. He who is master of himself possesses a gift which he will never wish to lose, which Fortune will never be able to take from him.

To know or to be ignorant of Fortune's fickleness

[1] " Nessun maggior dolore
Che ricordarsi del tempo felice
Nella miseria."
—Inf., v. 121.

is equally disastrous to the man on whom her favour
falls; for all ignorance implies unhappiness, and this
particular knowledge engenders gnawing fear. At
this point in the colloquy the divine physician
begins to apply her *remedia validiora*. What, she
asks, are Fortune's gifts, and which of them carries
happiness with it? Is it money? But money must
leave the purse before it can purchase felicity;
nothing is more graceless than avarice. Is it the
flash of jewels, or the beauty of the land and its
fruits? But no man can really claim these as his
own. Is it position and power? But the attain-
ment of these lies within the reach of the vilest of
mankind. And as nature abhors contraries, gifts
which fall to the lot of the wicked can have no
real good in themselves. Is it a great name? Here
Philosophy has laid her finger on a tender spot.
Yes, cries Boethius. I want scope for action, to
keep green and fresh the virtue that I know is in
me. It is then explained how narrow are the limits
of human glory. This earth is but a tiny speck in
the vast system of the universe: how contemptible
must the splendour of a single city, much more that
of one of its inhabitants, appear to him whose gaze
is familiar with the infinity of the heavens. In the
time of Cicero the fame of the Republic, then in its

flower, had not spread across the Caucasus; how "cribbed, cabined, and confined" must have been the renown of even its noblest citizen. Again, what one time and one nation looks upon with approval, another will unhesitatingly condemn. So a man must be content with a name bounded by his own epoch, and known to his contemporaries only. As to the glorious title of philosopher, it is one thing for a man to cheat himself into the belief that he is one, but quite another really to deserve the name. However, Philosophy has at the last a good word to say for Fortune. When that cruel goddess changes her deceitful smile to a frown, and in so doing proclaims her changeful nature, then she is indeed true; then, and then alone, can she lead men back to the only Good, from which she has lured them away in the time of their prosperity.

Book III.

The patient feels his strength returning under the inspiring words of Philosophy, and declares that he can support a yet further increase in the potency of her remedies. She thereupon leads him into a discussion of the supreme Good, and of the craving of humanity to attain to it. It is this that makes

them so eager for the superficial and fleeting pleasures of Fortune; the very diversity of their desires
—some seeking riches, others fame, and so on—
points to some sovereign Good which shall satisfy
every longing.

All men, even the most degenerate, are impelled
to seek Good, each in his own way, and with more
or less discernment.   But wherein lies the true
Good, the object of their aspirations ? Not in wealth,
for in the amassing of riches a man must needs rob
his neighbour.   Nor yet in an honourable position,
for the climbing to office involves the preliminary
humiliation of the canvass for votes.   Nor again
in power, for that is a possession surrounded with
intrigue and danger.   And assuredly it does not lie
in pleasure, for that implies servitude to the basest
of all things, the body.

All these are insufficient, and but fragmentary
parts of some great whole that contains them all.
Before entering on the search for this whole, the
Father of all must be invoked, without whose aid
no undertaking can come to a successful issue.
After the invocation follows the proof.   God is
good, for there is nothing better than He; nay, He
is the perfection of goodness, and therefore the true
Good must reside in Him.   But happiness has been

acknowledged to be the true Good. Therefore happiness resides in God, and is none other than God; for accident cannot be predicated of Him, nor can He, who is best of all, be separated from the true Good. Men can to a certain extent participate in happiness, and in virtue of that participation attain to divinity.

All creatures make for happiness, and therefore seek God. Evil, notwithstanding the paradox, has no real existence; for God, who can do all things, cannot do evil.

Book IV.

Boethius confesses the truth and beauty of his teacher's words, but complains that the chief cause of his doubt and misery is still untouched. The fact that the universe is under the rule of a just and all-powerful God only makes the presence of evil in the world the more strange and lamentable; for evil *does* exist, if it be in appearance only, and its votaries succeed and flourish, while the good are often oppressed. It would indeed be direful, replies Philosophy, if in a well-ordered household, with which God's universe may fitly be compared, vile vessels were honoured and precious vessels despised.

But this is not the case. If our previous arguments hold, then it must follow that the good are always powerful, the wicked always powerless; for it is the essential characteristic of impotency to fall short of or miss the object of its aim. Now, while all men alike are conscious of the impulse towards Good, the good alone can attain thereto, the wicked never; for they start with a misconception of its nature, and an ignorance of the roads by which it may be reached. True, they may obtain the thing which their inclination leads them to seek, but never the thing which they really desire; for that, we have seen, is Good.

Again, it is quite wrong to suppose that the wicked are ever rewarded. In the mere loss of Good they suffer the most terrible chastisement that can be inflicted; their very freedom to work wickedness is a further aggravation of their punishment, and if their eyes were not blinded and their understanding darkened, they would rejoice in every correction laid upon them as one step more out of the mire in which they are plunged. Even the power which Philosophy does not deny that they possess—of a certain kind— is born of impotency, for they have power only over evil, and that is less than nothing. Plato was right when he said [1] the wise alone have power to do

[1] Gorgias, 507c.

what they will; the wicked only arrive at the fulfilment of their inclination.

Nor is this all. The wicked cannot be said to
exist any more 'than evil exists, for that alone *is*
which keeps its nature and preserves its order. By
disobeying the natural impulse towards Good, the
wicked man has violated the law of his nature, and
is become nothing more than a dead body, the ruin
of a man that once was.

To return to the question of rewards and punishments, a threefold chastisement lies on the wicked,
—firstly, in the will, secondly, in the power to work
evil, and thirdly, in the accomplishment of the
same. How gladly would I see them relieved of
this burden, cries Boethius bitterly. It will disappear,
answers Philosophy, even sooner than you hope, or
they look for. For in the swift course of human
life there is nothing comes so late that the waiting
for it can appear long to an immortal soul. The
great hopes and lofty scaffolding of wickedness often
come down in unexpected ruin. But even supposing
no such limit be set to wickedness, still if, as we
believe, iniquity begets misery, a man must be ever
the more miserable the longer he lives in iniquity.
It is well for him that death comes quickly to put an
end at once to his wickedness and his wretchedness.

After Boethius has acknowledged the fairness of both premise and conclusion, his teacher goes on to establish the theory which has already been put forward that punishment is a real benefit to the wrongdoer. He puts a question concerning the future punishment of the soul, and it must be allowed that the answer he receives is exceedingly vague and indefinite. " Dost thou not reserve," he asks, " any other penalties for souls after the death of the body? " " Assuredly I do reserve very grievous ones, of which, in my opinion, some, whose object is to punish, are rigorous ; while others, whose object is to purify, are merciful. But I have no mind to speak now on this matter. "

These discussions naturally lead on to the subject of Fate and Providence. The divine Intelligence, enthroned in the citadel of its own simplicity, hath devised a method for directing the variable order of things. Contemplated in its sublime and pristine purity, this method is called Providence ; with regard to, and in connection with, the things it acts upon, it is what the wise men of old called Fate. In other words, Providence is the supreme Reason that orders all things ; Fate is the instrument which, in the hands of Providence, binds together all things, and keeps them each in its proper place. Providence holds all things in an equal embrace, however diverse, however numerous, they may be. Fate sets all things in motion, apportioning to them their convenient times, forms, and places. Fate is dependent on Providence and emanates from it, though the two are of very different character. It is by means of Providence that God assigns to everything that is to be done its stability and individuality. It is through Fate that He has His orders carried out at different seasons and in different ways. What the intermediary agents between Providence and Fate may be, Philosophy does not take upon herself to assert.

"Whether it be through certain divine spirits which wait on Providence that Fate is carried out, or by the soul, or by the submissive service of the whole of nature, or by the heavenly motions of the stars, or by angelic virtue, or by the varied skill of demons, or by some of these, or by all of them, that the chain of Fate is woven—this is certainly clear, that Providence is the motionless and simple mould of all that is to be, while Fate is the moving coil and temporal order of all that which the divine Simplicity has ordered to be carried out."

In proposing these alternatives, Philosophy only wishes to emphasise the immobility of Providence as distinguished from the flexibility of Fate. The

relation between these two is further illustrated by
the analogy of concentric circles. There are some
things which rise above the order of Fate; thus
those things which are firmly fixed close to the
divine Simplicity stand without the moving order
of Fate. That which lies farthest away from the
primary Intelligence is entwined in closer meshes of
Fate; and conversely, things are the more completely
freed from Fate, the nearer they approach the hinge
of all things. As reasoning is to the intellect, as that
which becomes to that which is, as time is to eternity, as the circle is to its centre, so is Fate in all
its moving succession to Providence in its motionless
simplicity. It is Fate that so rigidly binds together
cause and effect, that to our eyes there is sometimes an apparent confusion and misordering of
things. We must remember that there does exist
a method which directs and disposes all things for
good. Nothing is left to wilful chance—everything
is under the rule of Providence; and even those
things which have fallen out of the path marked out
for them, are directed into some other path by that
order which embraceth all things. Ἀργαλέον δέμε
ταῦτα θεὸν ὡς παντ' ἀγορεύειν, and it is not given
to man either to grasp with his intelligence or to
explain in words all the intricate machinery of God's

designs. Let us be content with our knowledge that
the same God who hath begotten all things doth
dispose and order them for good, and that, while
anxious to keep in His likeness all that He hath
brought into being, He driveth all evil, and all that
is unlike Him, beyond the bounds of His kingdom
by means of the order of fateful necessity.

As a final conclusion, Philosophy argues that all
fortune is good, since it only comes by God's good
will. The approach of that which is falsely called
ill-fortune should nerve the wise man to the fight—
that fight against either fortune in which all you
who are advancing towards virtue must engage;
against ill-fortune, lest it overwhelm you, against
good fortune, lest it undermine you. The middle
way between the two must be boldly seized and
held.

Book V.

The six sections in prose and five in verse of this
book are taken up with an elaborate discussion on
the compatibility of man's freewill with God's foreknowledge in a universe where nothing exists without its proper cause, and where all is under the rule
of a good and wise Governor.

But, asks Boethius, in all this rigid bond of cause

and effect is there no place for liberty of choice?
For if God knows all things and cannot be deceived,
that of necessity must come to pass which His prescience has foreseen. Thus freewill disappears and
necessity takes its place. Communion with Him
becomes impossible, prayer is rendered useless, for
how can an earthly demand affect the course of
things that have been already immutably fixed on
high? Philosophy's answer opens with a definition
of eternity, which, as distinguished from perpetuity,
is the whole and complete possession of intermina-
ble life, and this can be attributed to God alone
Nothing that suffers the condition of time, though it
neither ever began to be, nor should ever cease to
be (as in Aristotle's opinion was the case with the
world), nor yet though its life should stretch into
an infinity of time, can rightly be called eternal.
" And so if we would assign to things their proper
names, we shall say with Plato that God is eternal,
and that the world is perpetual." God, being
eternal, includes in His divine perception all things
that have happened, that are happening, and that
shall presently come to pass.

Just as our seeing a man walking does not lay
upon him any constraint to continue or to stop
walking, so this foreknowledge of God does not

necessitate the actions which it contemplates. It must be called Providence rather than Previdence, in order that no confusion may arise between the free-will of man and the divine ordering of the world.

But this very consciousness that all our thoughts and actions lie outstretched before God's all-seeing eye doth lay on man a certain necessity—a necessity so to live that nothing he can do or think may be out of tune with the divine harmony of His rule. "Wherefore the freedom of choice remains inviolate for mortal men; and those laws are not unfair which lay down rewards and punishments for wills bound by no necessity. Furthermore, there is One that looks down from on high, God, who hath foreknowledge of all things, the ever-present eternity of whose sight agrees with the future quality of our actions, assigning to the good reward, and punishment to the wicked. It is not in vain that we lay our hopes and prayers before God, for when they are right they cannot be without effect. Turn you from vice and ensue righteousness, uplift your mind to worthy hopes, in all humility direct your prayers to heaven. A strong necessity to live uprightly is laid upon you if you would not cheat yourself, since all your actions take place before the eyes of a Judge who seeth all things."

So ends the 'Consolation of Philosophy,' not, if I have read it aright, with any abrupt termination, as many have maintained, but rather with a serene and noble epilogue, which affords a grateful, and without doubt an intentional, contrast to the restlessness and petulance—for it is nothing less—that marks many passages in the earlier books.   Philosophy has kept her promise and fulfilled her mission.   She has raised her disciple gently and tenderly from the depths of depression and despair in which she found him to a calm and reverend trust in God.   She has shown him the emptiness of earthly things and the sovereign beauty of heavenly things; and there is no indication that Boethius had it in his mind to pursue the search for comfort any farther.   Nor does the fifth book betray any signs of haste or want of finish.   True, it falls short of the fourth book by some two hundred lines, and of the third by close on four hundred; but, on the other hand, it comes within thirty lines of the second, and is longer than the first by near a hundred; while the comparative infrequency of the songs and lyrics with which the writer is elsewhere so willing to vary his prose, only points to a feeling in his mind that metre was not the proper vehicle for the careful synthesis and ela-borate inductive development which was required

by so serious and unusual a subject as Freewill
and its compatibility with Providence. Indeed, he
has told us as much himself in a previous passage
(Cons. iv., pr. 6), where—the question under discussion being the relations between Fate and Providence—he puts these words into Philosophy's mouth :
" However much you may delight in the attractions
of music and poetry, you must put off that pleasure
for a little time while I weave a chain of orderly
connected arguments."

The peculiar form of mingled prose and verse in
which the ' Consolation ' is cast is known to scholars
as the *Satura Menippœa*, and takes its name from
the Cynic Menippus of Gadara (fl. 60 B.C.)

Terentius Varro, the herald of the Ciceronian age,
was the first among Latin authors to turn to account
Menippus's method, which was excellently suited to
his purpose—namely, a merciless and indiscriminate
exposure, from a cynical standpoint, of all existing
systems of philosophy. Varro's example was followed nearly a century later by the younger Seneca,
who employed the Satura Menippæa, not much to
his credit, for his scurrilous lampoon on the dead
emperor Claudius. In his 'Apokolakuntosis Claudii '
(the " Gourdification " of Claudius) the ungrateful
philosopher does his best to vilify the memory of a

benefactor for whom, when living, he had no words to express his admiration.

The satire seems to have had some vogue during the reign of Nero, for besides this diatribe of Seneca's, we meet with it in Petronius Arbiter's great farrago of wit, wisdom, and obscenity, of which the principal fragment remaining to us is the 'Cena Trimalchionis.'

Boethius borrowed nothing from these works beyond the hint for the literary form in which to clothe his moral and philosophical maxims. Nor was his debt considerable to his immediate predecessor in the Satura Menippæa, Martianus Capella (fl. 430 ?), whose extraordinary book 'De Nuptiis Mercurii et Philologiæ'—which, by the way, enjoyed an almost equal popularity with the 'Consolation' during the early middle ages—is marked by an extravagance and pedantry to which the later writer offers no parallel even in his least happy moments. It may, therefore, be safely claimed for our author that he was the first to apply the form of the old Greek medley to the serious treatment of philosophical questions,—that he was the first to invest it with any sort of dignity.[1]

[1] This account of the Satura Menippæa is mainly taken from Teuffel, Geschichte der Römische Literatur (1875), §§ 28, 3 ; 165, 3; 289, 7 ; 452.

Whereas his forerunners had heedlessly jumbled prose and verse, falling into the latter sometimes in the very middle of a sentence, he is careful to balance nicely the one against the other, choosing the moment with consummate art for the insertion of a song which shall carry on, and give emphasis to, the thoughts on which he has already exercised the full force of his pedestrian rhetoric and logical argument.

The regular appearance of poetry in the midst of a prose that (to us at least) is always difficult and sometimes dry, was doubtless intended to serve a double purpose : in the first place, to relieve the strain on the writer, without sensibly lowering the tone of the dialogue ; and secondly, to refresh the reader with a constant and agreeable variety. My excuse for dwelling at such length on the Menippæan Satire must be my conviction that the ' Consolation ' owed much of the popularity it afterwards enjoyed to the form in which its hard sayings were presented. Most men, when they are for reading philosophy, like to have it conveyed to them in as easy and intelligible a shape as possible.

No one will question the inferiority of Capella's work to that of Boethius, both in point of subject-matter and execution. And what is true of him is equally true of the other writers of the time, one and all. There is no doubt that Boethius brings us nearer to the Augustan age than any other Latin for three hundred years. To take his prose first. For all its affectation and excess of ornament,—I am here concerned with the 'Consolation' alone—it is temperate and simple in comparison with the bombast of Cassiodorus, which, in its turn, is infinitely preferable to the intolerable effusions of Ennodius. And yet these writers were reputed models of style, and on them fell the burden of the correspondence and literature of the court; while even Priscian, the famous Byzantine grammarian, betrays a strange unfamiliarity with good Latin.

If, then, we bear in mind how the intellectual vigour of the Latin race had been drained by three centuries of internal strife and corruption and deadly struggle with the barbarian; if we take into consideration the influence wrought by theological controversy, with its incessant demands for fresh terms with which to express thoughts that no writer of the golden age could ever have entertained—we shall be ready to forgive Boethius his occasional aberrations from the style of Cicero.

Obbarius has sagaciously remarked [1] that most of the expressions which offend an ear accustomed to

[1] *Op. cit.*, Proleg., i. 21.

the language of the Augustan period can be traced back to præ-classical authors. This tendency is not by any means peculiar to late Latin writers. A certain pedantry and archaic affectation is one of the commonest characteristics of every unspontaneous literature and art, and often follows as a natural reaction from the over-refinement and prejudice of a classical age. When we come to Boethius's verses, we feel at once that we are standing on surer ground. He displays an exceptional ingenuity and versatility in the employment of the various metres which he presses into the service of his Muse, and writes elegiacs, hexameters, asclepiads, sapphics, hendecasyllabics, and iambics, with equal address and correctness. His skill in this province of literature won the warm admiration of critics as fastidious as Casaubon and Julius Cæsar Scaliger, the latter of whom declared " quæ libuit ludere in poesi, divina sane sunt; nihil illis cultius, nihil gravius, neque densitas sententiarum venerem, neque acumen abstulit candorem. Equidem censeo paucos cum illo comparari posse." [1]

I do not suppose that the modern reader will be prepared to give an unqualified assent to this opinion of the great scholar of the Renaissance. But on the

[1] Poetices liber vi.

other hand, he will surely not be so unfair to our
poet as to say with Sitzmann that there is hardly a
verse in Boethius that does not seem to have been
taken from Seneca. Boethius has borrowed freely
from Nero's tutor, as Peiper's index at the end of his
edition of the 'Consolation' testifies; nor indeed did
he fail to lay Ovid and Horace, Virgil and Juvenal,
under contribution when it suited him. But while
he does not scruple to appropriate words and
phrases, and sometimes whole passages, from the
'Medea,' from the 'Hippolytus,' from the 'Hercules
Furens' and the 'Œtæus'—in fact, from nearly every
one of Seneca's plays in turn—he generally manages
to give them the impress of his own genius, and his
imitation is hardly of a kind to justify the old
German's hasty generalisation. He sometimes shows
a terseness and a brevity which are absent from the
work of the older poet. Take, for instance, the fifth
metrum of the second book ("Felix nimium prior
ætas"), and compare with it the descriptions of the
former age in the 'Medea' (301 *seqq.*), the 'Hippolytus'
(524 *seqq.*), and the 'Octavia' (390 *seqq.*),[1] where for
the same idea that Boethius expresses in thirty lines
Seneca employs seventy or eighty.

It is worthy of notice that the obligation of

[1] I quote from Farnabius's edition of the tragedies (London, 1624).

Boethius to his forerunners is most apparent in his treatment of mythological subjects; while in the metra of a purely philosophical character, such as iii. 9 and 11; v. 3 and 4, he owes nothing to any Latin poet. These at any rate show that he was quite able to walk alone. But there is a class of critic that takes a singular delight in running down similarities of expression in this and that artist. It should always be remembered that, as Mr Russell Lowell wisely says, the question of originality is not one of form but of substance; and that the greatest poets—Chaucer, Shakespeare, Molière—have been the most unblushing borrowers. Plagiarism, after all, is only blameworthy and in the nature of a crime, when the loan is not repaid with interest— when the imitation falls of the original; and a writer who can put a new dress on an old thought, though he may not lay claim to originality nor rise to true greatness, will always command the applause and gratitude of his fellow-men.

CHAPTER IV.

THE PHILOSOPHY OF THE ' DE CONSOLATIONE.'

Authorities. — Friederich Nitzsch, ' Das System des Boethius. Berlin, 1860. A. Hildebrand, ' Boethius und seine Stellung zum Christenthume.' Regensburg, 1885.

SECTION I.—GOD.

A THINKER of Boethius's mould and circumstances could not fail to be eclectic ; and his philosophical system is a mixture of Platonism (both in its original form and as Proclus and Plotinus taught it), Aristotelianism, and Stoicism. To begin with the influence exercised on him by the Attic philosopher, we see that his conception of God is purely Platonic. To be sure, we seem to trace the teaching of Christianity in his treatment of some of the divine qualities—for instance, God's prescience in relation

to man's freewill. The compatibility of human
freedom with a divine government of the world
was not a question that disturbed the older philosopher at all, who suffered to pass unchallenged the
apparent contradiction between that absolute freedom
of choice which he claimed for the soul, and the
involuntary character of vice and ignorance. But
those who are anxious to derive Boethius's theory
on this subject from a Christian source, are apt to
overlook the fact that it is already present in the
teaching of Proclus and the Neoplatonists. And
although Boethius is clearly out of sympathy with
these philosophers when they attempt to foist the
old heathen gods into their system as an offset
against Christianity, he has none of that uncompromising hatred of all that savours of Polytheism
that distinguishes the early Christian controversialists.

With characteristic caution he keeps the *via media*,
and in a highly significant passage (iv. 6, 51) ex-
hibits a complete indifference as to the agency by
which the divine commands are put in execution.
But he is careful not to fall into the Charybdis of
Pantheism in avoiding the Scylla of Polytheism—
that is, as far as the Physic of the Stoics is concerned. Such expressions as *naturæ anima* (iii. m.
9), *natura rerum* (i. pr. 5 ; iii. pr. 4), are not the

utterance of a disciple of the Porch (whose all-
pervading principle was immanent in nature), but
are taken straight from the 'Timæus'—indeed the
ninth metre of the third book is, in Nitzsch's words,
nothing but *ein ganzer Abschnitt des Timaeus ver-
sificirt*—and his natural law is simply the expression of the will of a transcendental God, who is
over and above the world, the only Father of things,
the producer of all natures.

On the other hand, phrases of this kind—and
they abound—are very far from landing him on
Christian territory. His " Father " of all things
is a purely physical conception — the πατὴρ τοῦδε
τοῦ πάντος of the 'Timæus,' and something very
different from the loving Father of the New
Testament. But the Deity of the 'Consolation' is
a much more definite being than the Deity of Plato's
dialogue, who is merged in the Ideas which served
Him as a copy for His universe; and although it
would not be difficult to find passages both in the
'Timæus' and elsewhere to match the kindly firmness, the perfect knowledge, the righteous wrath, the
care for His creatures, which Boethius attributes to
God, there would seem to be no doubt that the
Roman philosopher had a clearer notion than the
Greek of God's personal existence. Thus he does

not shrink from the expression "to converse with
God,"—*colloqui cum Deo*,—in speaking of the necessity
and efficacy of prayer. It must be owned that such
personal epithets as *præsens* and *amicus*, if not strictly
Platonic, are applied to the Deity by both Cicero
('Tusc.,' i. 27) and Seneca ('De Prov.,' i. 44; ii. 6).
Our philosopher, however, returns to Plato when
he speaks of God as *livore carens* (iii. m. 9); and
his use of the word "love" in such phrases as *cælo
imperitans amor* (ii. m. 8) and *æternus et cunctis
communis amor* (iv. pr. 6) is an echo of the φίλια of
Empedocles, conveyed to us through the medium of
the 'Timæus.' It is the concord that keeps the
universe together, and has no sort of connection
with the ἀγαπή of St John's Gospel.

SECTION II.—THE UNIVERSE.

Although neither the χώρα of Plato nor the
ὕλη of Aristotle bear much resemblance to the
dualism of Mani, still both one and the other philosopher were manifestly embarrassed by the existence
of matter. It is now necessary to determine what
position Boethius assumed with regard to this question; and here if anywhere we have a crucial test
by which the Christianity of our author must stand

or fall. The Christian revelation distinctly states that " in the beginning God created the heaven and the earth." Now Boethius quotes with approval the axiom " ex nihilo nihil "; and while he is careful not to include the efficient cause within the limits of this precept, he gives his emphatic assent to it as far as concerns the material substrate, and his thoughts seem to dwell with affectionate regret on the blissful days of philosophy when no one ventured to dispute its truth—" nam nihil ex nihilo existere vera sententia est cui nemo umquam veterum refragatus est " (v. pr. 1). Such an expression of regret would be impossible on the lips of an earnest student of the Bible. He goes on to develop the theory of the world's origin, not in any Christian spirit, but wholly under the influence of Aristotle.[1] Thus God is not only the cause but the end of all things (iii. pr. 12). All creatures naturally seek a sovereign Good—seek happiness. This impulse often takes a false direction, making them pursue some part of Good, such as wealth or fame or friendship, and fall short of that Good which is One, and comprises all the rest.

This highest Good or sovereign happiness must exist in reality, and not merely reside in the imag-

[1] Cf. Nic. Ethics, Bk. i., *passim.*

ination;[1] the presence of an incomplete Good or of an imperfect happiness, which we know by experience is always with us, argues a complete Good, a perfect happiness, for it is not possible that the complete should grow out of the incomplete, but *vice versâ*.

We see here that Boethius does not attempt to prove the existence of God, but rather the existence of a perfect Good which must be identical with God. He does not start with the idea of completeness, and work out from it a proof of God's existence; he takes the existing incomplete as his point of departure. In a word, the implicit proof of God's existence is cosmological, and very different from the ontological proof put forward by Augustine. Over and above this proof there is the physico-theological proof, as Nitzsch points out, referring to the passage in iii. pr. 12, where Boethius gives the name of God to that something without which the created world could not hold together, nor be set in motion.

Once again, the attributes of inaccessibility (v. pr. 3), simplicity (v. pr. 6), and purity (iv. pr. 6), which he predicates of his Divinity, are not drawn from the Christian vocabulary. " The eternal God

[1] Cf. Nic. Ethics, Bk. i. c. 6.

possesses and embraces in one instant the fulness of eternal life;" "In Him is life immovable;" "He sits enthroned in the citadel of His simplicity;" —expressions like these recall to one's mind the mental position of a Proclus rather than that of an Augustine.

Augustine had won his way by the spiritual experience of a lifetime to the clear knowledge of One who is absolutely good, who is absolute Unity, whom he could nevertheless approach and apprehend. Proclus's primary object was to keep God apart from the world of His creation. He is a pure, inaccessible, simple Essence,[1]—exactly the phraseology of Boethius, be it remarked,—and the Creator must be inferior to ἕν in so far as concerns the predication of energy and working power. To the same origin must be referred the *dæmonum varia sollertia* which Boethius speaks of as a possible intermediary agency between Providence and Fate, mentioning in the same breath with it *angelica virtus*, which is as certainly a trace of Christian, as the former is of Neoplatonic, influence. It is clear that Boethius was acutely sensible of the difficulty Proclus felt about confounding the transcendental Essence with the created world; accordingly we find him taking his

[1] De Prov., 50-52.

predecessor's Fate as the intermediary, dependent
divinity, and his Providence as the primary Essence.
In considering this point the reader must be careful
to bear in mind the grand difference between the
Neoplatonic and the Stoic doctrine of Fate.   The
disciples of the Porch looked upon εἱμαρμενή simply as one of the names of the all-pervading Principle, and identified it with Providence, πρόνοια,
while the Neoplatonists held it to be distinctly inferior to, and dependent on, Providence.   Boethius,
here as everywhere else, takes his stand somewhere
between the two extremes of opinion.   Proclus arranged his divinity in three grades—(1) Πρόνοια,
the pure Essence ; (2) Νοῦς, the divine creative Intelligence ; and (3) Εἱμαρμενή, which has the ordering of corporate and sensible things.   Our philosopher identifies Πρόνοια with Νοῦς, and assigns to
Εἱμαρμενή a higher place than that which it held in
the Neoplatonic system : for him it is the expression
of the divine Reason in its connection with the
created world.   The Stoics, as I have pointed out,
regarded all three as immanent in nature, and as
nothing but various titles of the Cosmic Soul.   This
naturally brings us to a closer consideration of God
in His relation to nature.   We have seen that
Boethius does not exclude from his system a cer-

tain substrate, that his *prima divinitas* did not " in
the beginning create " the world, but built it up[1]
from pre-existing matter.[2]   Impelled by no external causes, He ungrudgingly shaped it after His own
divine image, and taught it to carry out the scheme
of perfection in accordance with which it had been
formed.   Mutual love, *alternus amor*,[3] is the bond
that keeps the whole together, while every being,
under the impulse of a certain self-love implanted
in it by Providence, seeks to maintain its own independent entity.   Over all God sits enthroned, sur-
veying the work with serene, all - comprehending
eye, and fulfilling the promptings of His divine intelligence through the agency of Fate.   For the
time-relations between the Creator and the creation
Boethius goes back to the Platonic distinction between perpetuity and eternity, from which Proclus
and his followers had strayed through a misconception of 'Timæus,' 41*c*.   They imagined that Plato
assigned to the world a co-eternity with God, whereas he had only predicated of it a life of endless duration and not at all that simultaneous and complete
comprehension of all time which is the characteristic

---

[1] Cf. " Conditor et artifex rerum," i. m. 5.   Cf. also iv. pr. 6 ; iv.
m. 6.

[2] " Pepulerunt fingere causæ materiæ fluitantis opus "—iii. m. 9.

[3] The φιλία, *i.e.*, of Empedocles and of the Timæus.

of eternity. Boethius lays great stress on the incompleteness of the world, which can only afford to mortals a semblance of the true Good (*imagines veri boni*), inasmuch as having once *become*, it cannot last for ever (iii. pr. 9). Over and above these limitations to the completeness of the physical world, he mentions three agencies—Fortune, Chance, and Evil —which appear to restrict the sovereign rule of God in nature.

Section III.—Fortune.

I say intentionally " appear to restrict," because he loses little time in stripping these forces of all reality. For instance, Fortune, which he distinguishes from Fate, is merely an instrument in God's hand for the correction and education of man, and however harmful and capricious she may appear to his limited intelligence, she is really good in whatever guise she comes.

Section IV.— Chance.

Again, Chance, he tells us, far from being something that wilfully violates the divine order, is rather the fulfilment of one side of that order. If it were in no wise bound by a chain or sequence of causes,

it could have no existence at all, for " *ex nihilo nihil.*"
Chance is, according to Aristotle's definition, " the
unexpected event of an action brought about by a
confluence of causes foreign to the object proposed."
Now these concurrent and confluent causes are the
effect of that order which proceeds by a necessary
sequence, and, taking its rise in Providence, assigns
to each and all their proper time and place.

SECTION V.—EVIL.

To the mind of Boethius evil is what it was to
the mind of Plato, nothing but a shadow and a semblance ; for God, who can do all things, cannot do
evil. How, then, can evil exist ? Certainly experience teaches us that something that we call physical evil is present with us, but, far from being evil
in reality, it is an instrument for good, and its inflic-
tion is the greatest benefit that can be conferred upon
the wicked.[1] Moral evil, however, presents a difficulty different in kind and in degree from physical
evil, and the arguments advanced by Boethius to dis-
prove its reality are somewhat feeble and common-
place. Thus, he speaks of the victims of moral evil
as non-existent, as mere moral corpses, not seeing

[1] Cf. Prot., 323, 4 ; Gorg., 472, 3 ; 477 ; 479 ; 508 ; 523 ; 525.

that the power to strike dead or wither implies a
certain lively vigour and reality.

Although he seems to be so far in accord with
Christian doctrine that he looks upon moral evil as
in no way limiting God's goodness, and on sin as the
fruit of man's own wilful disobedience and free
choice, as a disease of the soul and nothing more,[1]
still he is very vague and doubtful on this point,
and chooses rather to confess the wickedness of the
majority of mankind than to include, with Augustine,
the whole world in one sweeping condemnation.
Indeed, he recognises the possibility of man's attain-
ing to perfection, and that without any assistance
from divine grace. The notion of a world lost in
sin and in need of a Redeemer is one that does not
suggest itself to him at all.

SECTION VI.—PSYCHOLOGY OF THE 'CONSOLATION.'

The stoical conception of the soul as a blank tablet
which receives external impressions from the material world, finds no place in Boethius's psychology.
On the contrary, he dismisses it with contempt and
opprobrium, and adopts in its stead the Platonic
doctrine of Ideas at rest within the soul, which only

---

[1] "Ad iudicium veluti ægros ad medicum duci [sc. improbos]
oportebat, ut culpæ morbos supplicio resecarent."

need the quickening power of sensible perception to
arouse them. In developing this portion of his
scheme Boethius adheres to the time-honoured division of science into sense, imagination, reason, and
intelligence. Man is a rational and mortal creature,
akin to God through his reason and understanding.
Although he may become like God in virtue of his
powers of reason, he may never hope to attain to
that intelligence which is the peculiar characteristic
of the Deity; sense and imagination are both of
them subject to reason—nay, they are absolutely dependent on it for their very existence. At this
point we seem to catch upon the air the faint pre-
monitory sounds of the great battle of the middle-
age philosophy, the controversy between the Nomi-
nalists and Realists. It will be the business of a
later chapter to discuss the nature of the point dis-
puted, and to inquire more particularly into the position our author occupies with regard to the rival camps.
I fancy he will be found halting somewhere between
them, uncertain with which of the two to cast his
lot. The influence of Plato, which it is easy to see
was strong upon him as he wrote the 'Consolation,'
inclined him to declare in favour of Realism in that
book; but he only touches lightly on the question,
and recourse must be had to other writings of his,

notably the two commentaries on the 'Isagoge' of
Porphyry, before a definite opinion can be formed
one way or the other.

"The soul is of divine origin,[1] and it is upon
a constant communion with the divine elements of
knowledge that all its science and knowledge de-
pend.[2] By an inborn impulse it is led to seek Good,
though in many cases it falls short of its goal
through weakness, misconception of its duty (iv. pr.
2), or contact with the material body.[3] Now the
highest Good is God, and he who attains to the Good
becomes in a measure divine through participation."

The road by which this highest Good is to be
reached is not very clearly indicated.

"... e cælo descendit γνῶθι σεαυτόν,"

wrote Juvenal; and although Boethius does not
actually cite the Delphic maxim, he implies assent
to it by his remarks on the ends which are set
before humanity. A man's first duty is to know

[1] Cf. "Hic [i.e., Deus] clausit membris animos celsa sede
petitos"—iii. m. 6.

[2] If iii. m. 9 is founded on the Timæus, v. m. 3 may claim a
Platonic origin with equal right. The theory of reminiscence, which
is the prominent theme of the Meno, is closely reproduced—e.g.,

> " Sed quam retinens meminit summam
> Consulit alte visa retractans
> Ut servatis queat oblitas
> Addere partes."

[3] "Obruta mens cæcis membris"—v. m. 3. Cf. iii. m. 6; iv. m. 7, &c.

himself in order that he may shortly become convinced of the utter worthlessness of external goods (ii. pr. 5 and 6). He must conquer Fate; he must free his soul from the fetters of the body and let it soar to heaven on the wings with which Philosophy will fit it, calling the while on God to help him in his effort to rise above the earth (v. pr. 3 and 6).

This, then, is the ethic of Boethius,—to seek the highest Good in God, to lead a pure life, knowing that every movement and every deed takes place in His eternal presence.

The thought is noble, the words are not wanting in inspiration, but no one surely will have the hardihood to maintain that either thought or expression are particularly Christian. A moment's consideration of his doctrine of evil will bring this out into stronger relief. To it, as has been said above (p. 91), he denies all real existence, and so precludes the necessity of redemption for sinful man; for sin brings its own punishment with it, and passion has power to weaken but not to destroy.[1] Wickedness is a sickness of the soul which should move our pity rather than our indignation.

[1] Contrast "convellere sibique totum [hominem] exstirpare non possunt" (i. pr. 6) with "timete eum qui potest et animam et corpus perdere in gehennam"—Matt. x. 28.

Section VII.—Freewill and Predestination.

This theory of sin, so different from the Christian doctrine of original sin, brings us by a natural transition to freewill, which belongs to all intelligent beings by right of their reason and power of discernment. All, however, do not possess it in an equal degree, for while heavenly substances are endowed with unrestricted freedom of choice and an incorruptible will, human souls hold these gifts in varying proportion, according as they rise above the material to the spiritual. Sometimes they are too weak for the burden, and then, losing all intelligence, they sink and become involved in chains of deepest slavery (v. pr. 2).

Theorising such as this flows straight from the Platonic spring, and one would search long and vainly through the library of Christian philosophy to find its equivalent there.

It has already been seen (p. 71) how Boethius tried to reconcile human freewill with divine prescience by comparing and contrasting God's knowledge of that which is to be with our knowledge of that which is. In support of his argument he takes as examples the fulfilment of some natural law, as the sun rising, or the performance of some obvious

act of freewill, as a man walking. It only remains for me to point out that the solution of this
problem is simply an amplification of the Platonic
and Neoplatonic doctrine. Proclus so far modified
the teaching of his master, as he found it in ' Phæd-
rus,' section 248, that he assigned to the soul either
an ethereal or an earthly body. But he went a step
further and predicated of it, even in pre-existence, a
body corporeal. Boethius, with his wonted discretion,
strikes a compromise, accepting Plato's incorporeal
soul *as well as* both the ethereal and the material
body with which Proclus clothed his souls, reserving
yet a lower grade for the soul that is blinded by sin.[1]
This side of Boethius's psychology deserves one word
more. He distinctly says (v. pr. 2) that man's immaterial spirit is most at liberty when it is employed
in the contemplation of the divine Intelligence : it
enjoys less freedom when it has entered into a body,
and still less when it is bound to earthly members,
the depth of slavery being reached when it gives
itself over to vice and loses sight of God (*vide
supra*, p. 94). We have here no Christian allegory

---

[1] We might possibly find here a recollection of Augustine's doctrine of the necessity laid on natural man, were it not for the con-
tradictory passage already quoted, p. 72, which savours too strongly
of Pelagianism.

—as Pierre Cally [1] would have us believe, rendering the *beatæ mentes* of Boethius by "souls in contemplation," and seeing in the other two classes a reference to man's state before and after the fall—but simply an extension ₁ of the Platonic theories I have just been discussing.

The scheme of reward and punishment laid down in the fourth book of the 'Consolation' speaks for itself and needs scarcely any comment.   No one can fail to be struck with the Stoical ring of these passages : "studium ad peiora deflexens, extra ne quæsieris ultorem ; infeliciores eos esse qui faciant quam qui patiantur iniuriam " (iv. pr. 4) ; [2] while the observations on punishment after death at once recall the 'Gorgias,' 525 B, and 'Phædo,' 113 D, though, indeed, the notion of "pœnalis acerbitas " is altogether foreign to Plato.

Catholic commentators like Suttner and Hildebrand are naturally disposed to lay stress on the "purgatoria clementia," and entirely overlook the passage in the 'Gorgias,' which is so significant that I may be excused if I reproduce it intact : εἰσι δὲ οἱ μὲν ὠφελούμενοί τε καὶ δίκην διδόντες ὑπὸ θεῶν τε καὶ

---

[1] In his edition of the Consolation, published in 1680 (Delphin).

[2] Cf. Juvenal, xiii. 1, *seqq.;* Seneca, De Ira, ii. 30, 2; iii. 26, 2.

'ανθρώπων οὗτοι οἱ ἄν ἰάσιμα ἁμαρτήματα ἁμαρτῶσιν·
ὅμως δὲ δι' ἀλγηδόνων καὶ ὀδυνῶν γίγνεται αὐτοῖς ἡ
ὠφελεῖα καὶ ἔνθαδε καὶ ἐν Αἴδου· οὐ γὰρ οἷόν τε ἄλλως
ἀδικίας ἀπαλλάττεσθαι.[1]

It now remains to be seen what are our philosopher's views on the resurrection of the body, that
sheet - anchor of fifth - century theology. He undoubtedly believes in an immortality, as his allusions
to punishment after death declare, but he only admits,
with Plato, the immortality of the soul. The ethereal
body, which he borrows from Proclus, applies only
to the pre-existence of the soul, and there is not a
word to warrant our extending it to the dead, or
identifying it with the spiritual body of 1 Cor.
xv. 44, *seqq.* And such a material resurrection
as both Jerome and Augustine looked for would
have shocked his metaphysical habit of mind; for
however practical and dialectical Boethius shows
himself in his other earlier writings, in the ' Consolation ' he is chiefly concerned with the search after
an ideal which shall lift him out of himself.

We have now come to the end of our survey of
the philosophical system of Boethius, and must
pause a moment to gather up the threads that will

[1] Cf. Thompson's note on this passage, and therewith Seneca,
Cons. ad Marc., cap. 25.

lead us out of the labyrinth. It is often well to call in the aid of synthesis at the close of a process of analytical inquiry.

The system of the ' Consolation ' may be succinctly described as Platonic, modified by Aristotelianism ; and as a Roman of Boethius's tastes and education could not help having an intimate knowledge of Cicero and Seneca, there is nothing surprising in the strong dash of Stoicism that tinges the whole. But while he often echoes the doctrines of Proclus and Plotinus, he studiously avoids any attempt to blend Christ with Plato, such as was made by Synesius and the pseudo-Dionysius in the fifth and sixth centuries.

We find him in strenuous opposition—notwithstanding all that Hildebrand has to say to the contrary [1]—to the Christian theory of creation, and his Dualism is at least as apparent as Plato's. We find him coquetting with the anti-Christian doctrine of the immortality of the world, and assuming a position with regard to sin which is ultra-Pelagian and utterly untenable by a Christian theologian. We find him, with death before his eyes, deriving consolation not from any hopes of a resurrection, of seeing God in this flesh, but from the present con-

[1] *Op. cit.*, pp. 86-94.

tempt of all earthly pain and ill which his divine
mistress, " the perfect solace of wearied souls," has
taught him.

And certain expressions which are looked upon
by some commentators as so many finger-posts,
scattered up and down throughout the five books
with careful carelessness, and pointing to an intention in the writer's mind rather Christian than otherwise, prove on closer inspection to be but false guides.[1]
Let us examine them one by one.

(*a*) " Purgatoria clementia " (iv. pr. 4). This I
have already dwelt on long enough (*vide supra*,
p. 98), and may pass on without further remark
to—

(*b*) " Quo vero quisquam ius aliquid in quempiam,
nisi in solum corpus, fortunam loquor, possit exercere "
(ii. pr. 6). Here we have, not a reminiscence of
Matt. x. 28, " Fear Him which is able to destroy
both body and soul," but simply an abridgment of
Seneca's words, " errat siquis existimat servitutem in
totum hominem descendere . . . pars meliora . . .
excepta est . . . corpus itaque quod domino fortunæ tradidit " (Sen., De Benefic., iii. cap. xx.) [2]

---

[1] It is only fair to say that Hildebrand recognises the truth of all
the ensuing points.

[2] Cf Sen., Cons. ad Helv., cap xi. *ad finem*.

(c) "Tulit crimen iniqui justus" (i. m. 5). Our thoughts naturally go back to "the just for the unjust," but Boethius is here merely enlarging on the unrighteous sentence passed on himself.

(d) "Iam vos secunda mors manet (ii. m. 7). The "mors secunda" of which he sings refers to the loss of renown; it may indeed be compared for the thought with Eccles. ix. 10 : "Quodcunque facere potest manus tua, instanter operare; quia nec opus, nec ratio, nec sapientia, nec scientia erunt apud inferos, quo tu properas"; but certainly not with θάνατος ὁ δεύτερος of the Apocalypse.

(e) "Huc omnes pariter venite capti quos ligat fallax . . . libido." (iii. m. 10). These remarkable words appear at first sight to have been, and very possibly were, suggested by the Sermon on the Mount. But though the wording is similar, the feeling is very different.

(f) "Est igitur summum bonum, quod regit cuncta fortiter, suaviterque disponit" (iii. pr. 12). This is strangely like Wisd. viii. 1 : "Attingit vero a fine usque ad finem fortiter et disponit suaviter"; indeed it is altogether too like to be anything but a remin- iscence. But just as in the last quotation, so here, similarity of expression by no means implies identity of thought. And if we regard Boethius as a Christian by outward profession at least, there is nothing surprising in such echoes of Scripture. It is rather a cause for wonder that in the last utterance of a writer whom we believe to have produced serious disquisitions on subtle points of Christian doctrine, such echoes are not far more frequent.

(g) " Nam ut quidam me quoque excellentior ait : ἄνδρος δὴ ἱέρον δέμας αἴθερες οἰκοδομῆσαν " (iv. pr. 6). Many and various have been the conjectures offered as to who this "some one more excellent than Philosophy" can be—almost as numerous as the attempts at emending the manifestly corrupt text.[1] Sources as wide apart as Hermes Trismegistus and God speaking to us by the mouth of Christian Theology have been suggested—this last by Hildebrand (op. cit., p. 141), who, while he despairs of hitting on the right reading, declares the thought to be Christian. Now to my mind both thought and expression appear thoroughly Platonic, and Hildebrand's arguments to the contrary altogether unsatisfactory. There is a passage in the Second Alcibiades, § 292, which bears a remarkable resemblance to the words in question. Socrates says : Ἆρ' οὖν οὐχὶ εἰδώς τι πλέον ἡμῶν ὁ

---

[1] *Vide* Peiper's critical note on the passage. The "quidam me excellentior" he does not hesitate to identify with Parmenides, and compares Parm. περὶ φύσεως, 116 and 146, *seqq.*

ποιητής, οὗ καὶ ἐν ἀρχῇ τοῦ λόγου ἐπεμνήσθην, τὰ δεινὰ καὶ εὐχομένους ἀπαλέξειν ἐκέλευεν; [1]

The phraseology, indeed, does recall that of Ps. xxxiv. 20, Wisd. iii. 1, &c., just as the " vasa vilia et vasa pretiosa " of iv. pr. 1 recall the words of St Paul in 2 Tim. ii. 21, and the " Huc omnes pariter venite " of iii. m. 10, the words of Christ in Matt. xi. 28. And we should perhaps explain them as an unconscious reminiscence of familiar expressions, whose original application Boethius was not particularly careful to bear in mind. It is significant that he always acknowledges a debt to Plato or Aristotle : even in places where he does not mention them by name, the teaching of the Academic or of his great pupil is framed in language that leaves no shadow of a doubt as to the source from which it springs.

The circumstances of Boethius's life make it almost impossible to believe that he was other than a professing Christian before he fell in disgrace. How can this profession be reconciled with the system we have just been examining—a system which, while it is not directly antagonistic to Christianity, bears the impress of absolute indifference to it ? The general opinion on the subject may be roughly divided into

[1] Since writing the above, I have seen a note by Mirandol in his translation (Paris, 1861), where this passage of Plato is quoted.

two classes. First, there are those for whom the
'Consolation' is an insurmountable obstacle to the
theological tracts; secondly, there are those who
accept the tracts and regard the 'Consolation' as a
sort of palinode, the notification of the writer's final
withdrawal from the Christian faith. I shall reserve all argument with the former of these classes
until the tracts come under consideration. The
other view makes it exceedingly difficult to account
for such an unusual change of front. We should
have to believe that Boethius felt that after all,
logic, whether applied to questions of metaphysic
or theology, was but cold comfort in the prison-cell
or on the scaffold; and so explain the pronouncedly
Platonic turn his philosophy takes in the 'Consolation,'
after having been based on Aristotle hitherto, and
fostered by a constant worship of dialectic. We
must then class Boethius with those hearers of the
Word whom our Lord likened to the stony ground
on which the blessed seed falls, who have no root in
themselves, and stumble under the stroke of persecution. One could better have understood an open
attack on the religion that has profited him so little—
some fierce revulsion against a faith that failed him
so utterly in his hour of need. Now there seems to
me to be an alternative explanation at once simpler

and more in accord with common experience. The 'Consolation' is intensely artificial. Every page of it smells of the lamp. The verses in it have the smoothness and polish of marble, but they have also its coldness. Here is nothing that suggests a heart beating itself out against the bars of its prison. The prose, though it sometimes rises to a certain height of passion, often stiffens into the dull formality of a logical treatise. So, too, many of the themes elaborated, the tricks of Fortune, the misery of the wicked, and the like, are hardly of a kind to lead one to look on the work as a definite statement of ultimate religious conviction. There is really little depth of argument in the earlier books, and the later ones are in the main rather speculative than devout.

Bearing all this in mind, let us now see what Boethius was doing when Philosophy entered to him. He was writing poetry to pass the time and ease his pain. This, to my thinking, gives the clue to the motive of the 'Consolation.' The gloom and silence of the dungeon, the terrible consciousness of desertion by his friends, the enforced idleness, would have driven any ordinary man mad, much more one of Boethius's vast mental activity and insatiate appetite for work. He tries verse-writing, but finds that it

does him more harm than good leaving him exhaus-
ted and unstrung; his present excited mood is not
the one for theology; a philosophical dialogue with
occasional interludes of song shall be his diversion,
and help him to bear the ghastly companionship of
his own thoughts. Whenever his bitterness over-
masters him and he is giving way to the sense of his
wrongs, he can call in a physician who will enable
him to pause and look dispassionately on the uncertainty of human wishes and his miserable state;
who will brace his faculties, and perhaps recover for
him something of his ancient skill in reasoning.
This consummation is certainly reached towards the
end of the dialogue, where the pupil proves himself
by no means unequal to the severe catechetical
discipline to which his mistress subjects him. But
the passages where the writer lets his heart speak
and gives his brain a rest, of which the fine perora-
tion to the fifth book is a notable example, show
that Boethius, had he chosen, might have touched a
chord within us which no amount of logical thrust
and parry can set vibrating.

Whatever the motive of the 'Consolation' may have
been, it remains a very noble book, and is, for me at
least, by far the most interesting example of prison
literature the world has ever seen.

CHAPTER V.

THE THEOLOGICAL TRACTS.

Authorities.—Hildebrand and Nitzsch, as before. The analysis of each treatise has been made straight from the Latin text in Peiper's edition.

WE now come to the religious writings of Boethius —that side of his versatile genius which will, I fear, prove the least attractive to the general reader. But although their intrinsic value may not be of the very highest, although they betray many faults of youth and inexperience (I have heard them described as so many Hulsean essays!), still they have a distinct interest attaching to them as coming, if we believe the 'Anecdoton Holderi' and the almost unbroken tradition of the middle ages, from the same hand that wrote the 'Consolation of Philosophy,' and as forming one more link in the chain that connects Boethius with the Schoolmen.

The best way of bringing out this interest will be, I think, to give a careful analysis of them, in order as they come, preserving just so much of their original form and style as will illustrate the author's method, and keeping back all detailed criticism of their respective merits and shortcomings until the survey of each one is finished.

There are five tracts generally ascribed to Boethius, and this is the order in which they almost invariably appear in the MSS. :—

I. De Trinitate.

II. Utrum Pater et Filius et Spiritus Sanctus de Divinitate substantialiter prædicentur.

III. Quomodo Substantiæ bonæ sint.

IV. De Fide Catholica.

V. Liber contra Eutychen et Nestorium.

This list corresponds very well with that of the 'Anecdoton Holderi' and with the testimony of Alcuin (735-804) and Hincmar of Rheims (ninth century), the former of whom makes mention of I. and quotes from it,[1] while the latter was evidently familiar with I., II., and V. Bruno of Corvey (tenth century) ascribes I. and V. to Boethius. Notker of St Gall (†1022) translated passages from I. Haimo (tenth century) couples I. with the

---

[1] *Vide supra*, p. 2.

'Consolation'; and Abelard (✝1142) gives praise to
Boethius's books on the Trinity and against Nestorius.
The evidence of the succeeding ages is of secondary
importance, as it is simply a reiteration of the above.
Suffice it to say that until the beginning of the last
century the authenticity of the dogmatic treatises
remained practically unchallenged.

Having said so much, I will proceed to the analysis of—

I.—DE TRINITATE.

It opens with a preface addressed, according to
the consensus of MSS. titles, to his dear friend and
father Symmachus, in which the writer confesses the
interest he has for some time past taken in certain
difficult questions of doctrine.   Their truth, indeed,
has already been established by Augustine, but he
hopes to throw some further light on them by means
of his logical training.   These few pages are intended
for his critic's eye alone, and not for the crude, un-
appreciative judgment of the general public.   He
begs him to read them in the same spirit as that in
which they have been written.   No man may hope
to attain perfection.   He has done his best, and can
do no more.

Chapter i.—The Catholic faith on the Holy Trinity

in Unity is this. The Father is God, the Son is God, and the Holy Ghost is God. Therefore Father, Son, and Holy Ghost are one God, and not three Gods.

Now the Arians, who usurp the name of the Catholic religion, ascribe grades to the Persons, and so introduce plurality into the divine Substance. For the essence of plurality is difference. Three or more things can differ (1) by race (*genus*), (2) by kind (*species*), (3) by number (*numerus*). Diversity of accidents is the cause of the difference by number. Thus three men do not differ by race or by kind, but only by their accidents; and in the absence of all other accidents there will always remain the accident of place. Therefore accidents are the cause of plurality.

Chapter ii.—The speculative sciences are three in number—viz., *Physics*, which employ rational methods, and comprise those things which have motion and whose form is separated from their matter neither by abstraction (as in mathematics) nor in reality; *Mathematics*, which employ systematic methods (*disciplinaliter*), and comprise things which have no matter and therefore no motion; and *Theology*, which employs intellectual methods (*intellectualiter*), and deals with the absolute pure form at once immaterial and motionless—in other words, with the divine

Substance. All being depends, not on matter, but
on the form which is imprinted on it. For example, a statue is called a statue, not on account of
the bronze of which it is cast, but because of the
form it has received; and the bronze is not called
bronze because of the earth of which it is made, but
because of the form imprinted on it. Finally, the
earth is not earth *quâ* formless matter, but *quâ* dry-
ness and weight. But the divine Substance is pure
form without matter. It *is* what it is, and is absolutely simple; other things not being what they are, for
each owes its being to the parts of which it consists.
Thus man is body *and* soul, not body *or* soul. In
part, then, he is not what he is. But that which
has no part is only one, and is what it is. That is
really *one*, also, wherein is no number, which has
no substrate, because it is pure form and subject to
no accidents; for it is the matter on which form is
imprinted that receives accidents.

Chapter iii.—The threefold repetition of " God " in
naming the Trinity does not involve number. For
there are two kinds of number—one with which we
enumerate, the other which resides in the things
enumerated. Of these two, the former always involves a certain plurality; the latter does not involve
any. When we name the same thing three times,

calling it each time by a different name, we do not
enumerate three different objects, but one and the
same object—as, *e.g.*, when we say *ensis, mucro,
gladius* (each of which words designates the same
object), or repeat thrice the word " sun." So we must
make mention of the divine Substance in a threefold
manner, but carefully avoid describing it as a threefold God, as do the Arians when they draw distinc-
tions of merit between the Persons, and thus destroy
the unity of the Godhead. The examples from
material objects given above prove that not every
repetition of a unit involves plurality, but they
do not prove that Father, Son, and Holy Ghost are
only different titles of God, as *ensis, mucro, gladius*, are only different names for one and the same
thing; for while Father, Son, and Holy Ghost are
indeed the same thing, the Father is not the same
person as the Son, &c. And here we are confronted
by another kind of plurality. We must be very
careful how the different predicates are referred to
God.

Chapter iv.—According to Aristotle there are ten
predicates — substance, quality, quantity, relation,
place, time, condition, position, passivity, and activity. The signification of each of these depends on
the subjects with which they are associated. In

connection with dependent natures they signify
partly real qualities, partly accidents. In connection with God, on the other hand, they assume an
altogether different meaning. God is substance, and,
to distinguish His nature from dependent natures,
we may say that He is beyond substance. That
which in man is an accidental quality, is in God an
essential, or rather a superessential, quality. Thus,
when it is said that God is just, a quality is indeed
attributed to Him; but in His nature, justice and
existence are identical. He is just, because He is.
Even the real attributes, which in connection with
dependent natures signify only a partial existence,
in connection with God signify a real and complete
existence. Time and place are not real attributes,
and so cannot be predicated of God at all. Whereas
we can say of a man that he came yesterday, of
God we must declare that He is, and is always. The
former is an accidental predicate; the latter signifies
existence in the past, in the present, and in the
future. This is equally applicable, so say the philosophers, to the stars and other immortal bodies. But
in connection with God this " always " expresses a
present quite different from the " now " of temporal
things. Earthly time is fleeting and enduring for a
little while; divine eternity is permanent and im-

movable. So, too, the category of place is no real attribute. True, we can say of a man that he is in the market, but that is an accidental and not a real attribute, like " white " or " long." Now God is not in any place, but all places are present to Him. The other accidentals do not concern Him in any way.

Chapter v.—The category of relation (*ad quid*) will not help us much to realise the absolute qualities of a thing ; some external must come to its assistance with which it may be compared. Now the nature of a thing is not altered by relation. Take, *e.g.*, the relative conceptions " master " and " slave." If you remove " slave," you remove at the same time the predicate of master, but the real nature of the subject remains the same as before. This may seem to apply equally well to the category of quality, but in reality it does not—*e.g.*, white loses its being when the quality of whiteness is taken from it. So, then, relative predicates do not affect the real nature or being of the thing with which they are associated. Relation, however, indicates a reference, not necessarily to something else, but sometimes to the same thing. For instance, if I approach a man on the right, he becomes left with regard to me without being left by nature ; if I approach him on the left, he becomes right with regard to me without being right by nature. He is right or left simply by my means.

If father and son, then, are relative predicates, and only differ from one another by their relation to one another, these predicates involve not a *real* but only a *personal* difference in God's nature. God did not become Father by the addition of something to His nature: the procreation of the Son was natural to Him.

Thus the three Persons are separated by no difference, but where there is no difference there can be no plurality, hence there must be unity. So is the unity of the Trinity established.

Chapter vi.—The Trinity is secured by the removal of simple unity through certain relations; the Unity is maintained through the absence of all diversity in the Divine nature.

Applied to God, then, relation signifies the relation which a being bears, not to something external, but to itself. It is true that such a relation is not to be found in our dependent natures; but that is due to *cognata alteritas.* We can only hope to comprehend this mystery by an exercise of simple intelligence (the divine instrument of understanding) and God's help.

Epilogue.—The writer anxiously awaits his critic's judgment on this his attempt to illustrate with logic and reason a position which involves the truth of the Faith. Prayer must make up for any deficiency in the work.

We have seen that the evidence of the MSS. and the tradition of the middle ages from the ninth century onwards both speak in favour of Boethius as the author of the tracts. The *onus probandi* therefore lies with those who impugn their genuineness, and I might rest satisfied with defending them against the attacks of such. But I hope with Hildebrand's aid to be able presently to show that they have, besides, certain positive claims on internal grounds to be considered the work of the Roman statesman.

The main objection to their Boethian origin is the ' Consolation ' itself, and the argument supporting the objection amounts to this,—that a man who, with death staring him in the face, turned for comfort to heathen philosophy, could not have written on points of Christian doctrine.

I hope I have shown with sufficient clearness that the ' Consolation ' is all too artificial to be looked upon as a serious confession of faith. But even to those who prefer to look upon it as such, who see

in it the sum of all Boethius's thought and aspiration,
the existence of these dogmatic chapters should not
cause offence.   It is surely both unfair and un-
reasonable to insist that all a writer's achievements,
however different in kind and date, should be
measured by the same rigid standard; and a change
of opinions, a modification of religious views, does
not involve a loss of identity.   We are at liberty,
it must be remembered, to assign to each and all of
the tracts whatever place we see fit in the list of
Boethius's works, and there is no reason to prevent,
but rather every reason to encourage, our putting
them at the outset of his career.

Secondly, it is urged that the writer of the 'De
Trinitate' displays a dependence on Augustine such
as we may not look for in Boethius.

But Boethius's genius was imitative rather than
initiative; and nothing if not dependent.   His best
energies were spent on the adapting the writings of
the Greek philosophers to the requirements of Roman
readers.   And if in philosophy he was content to
take his stand on Plato and Aristotle, why in theology should he be deemed too proud to stoop to ask
help of Augustine ?

Thirdly, we are told that we know of nothing in
the life of Boethius which could have led him to

take up arms in defence of the doctrine of the Trinity.

We know very little indeed of the life of Boethius, but there is no need to ransack his writings or those of his contemporaries for the motive of the tract before us. His reasons for writing on the great Christian mystery are given as clearly as words can speak at the beginning of chap. v. : " Age nunc de relativis speculemur pro quibus omne quod dictum est sumpsimus ad disputationem."

The application of the Aristotelian predicate " relative " to the Godhead—this was the object he had in view. Whether he attained this end or fell short of it shall shortly be discussed.

Fourthly, " this tract has no polemical or practical tendency, such as is never absent from all disquisitions of that time on the Trinity. Arianism, on the contrary, is treated from a merely antiquarian point of view, suitable to a century later than the sixth."

Because we possess controversial treatises of the fifth and sixth centuries on the Trinity, shall we therefore say that there could not be one of that date written in an uncontentious spirit ? The answer to the preceding objection covers this one also. Boethius had it not in his mind to defend the Chris-

tian religion against the onslaught of any particular
heresy, but simply wished to illuminate it by logic
and exact reasoning. There was indeed no call for
him to undertake the duties of an Œcumenical Council—no fresh schism which demanded a fresh declar-
ation of the Faith. For Arianism, although it was
not yet crushed out of existence, only lingered on
among the barbarians—the Vandals in Africa and
the Goths in Italy—who were moved more from
policy than of conviction to continue their opposition to the Nicene Creed. Theodoric's reign had
been a model of toleration, and it cannot have
been until years after the composition of this
tract that his abortive attempt to persecute the
Catholics took place. The Eastern Church had
long been at rest from the fierce disputes that
distracted it under Valens; and Augustine, with
his 'De Trinitate,' had finally dispelled the difficulties that veiled the Trinity in Unity from the
minds of the Western Fathers, whose vision was
not so clear in the contemplation of the mystical
side of Christianity as that of their more imaginative
oriental brethren.

Fifthly, the style is said to be different from that
of Boethius, its only point of likeness lying in its
scholastic colouring. Now although I do not think

that much stress can be laid on similarity of style
where there is any suspicion of forgery or imitation, yet the ' De Trinitate ' has much in common
with the other authentic writings of Boethius.
Nitzsch himself, although it is he that puts forward this objection, admits that the *Schreibart*
of the pseudo-Boethius is not unlike that of the
real man.   There are, of course, expressions in the
tract that must jar upon the sensitive student of
the Golden Age; but even the pages of the ' Consolation,' which bears signs of such careful elabora-
tion, and is written in better Latin than had appeared at Rome for many a long year, are full of
barbarisms.

The Roman idiom, for which this critic says the
author has no feeling, seems to me to be not altogether absent from the Introduction, while it would
hardly find much scope in so unclassical a subject as
the predicaments in their application to God.   The
strangeness of most of the terms is excused by the
necessity laid upon the writer to give expression
to entirely new thoughts.   That Boethius did not
hesitate to experimentalise in this way, is seen from
his First Dialogue on Porphyry.

Besides these main objections, there are one or
two isolated phrases to which Nitzsch takes par-

ticular exception. The most noticeable of these is the sentence, " Ad aliquid vero omnino non potest prædicari " (*sc.* de Deo), which, if it be not a gloss, as Nitzsch himself suggests, does certainly expose the writer to the charge of obscurity and confusion, when he is presently discovered discussing the manner in which Relation can be predicated of the divine Essence. But the confusion is due, not to a momentary forgetfulness or want of logic on the writer's part, but to the radical defect of his work. Any attempt to apply the categories to God must end in disaster ; and although Boethius struggles manfully with them, and tries to simplify matters by postulating a twofold relation— 1, that of one thing to another, *ad aliquid ;* and 2, that of a thing to itself—he is left after all at variance with Aristotle, whose definition of Relation is " that which is predicated of, or stands in relation to, something else." [1]

Another phrase upon which Nitzsch bases a substantial charge is the *secundum philosophos* of chap. iv. He submits that this is an expression which Boethius, himself a philosopher, would not have used. The objection does not seem to me to merit much remark. In the Introduction the writer had

[1] Categor., c. 7.

acknowledged the debt he owed to philosophy generally, and therefore saw no necessity for encumbering
his little book with the list of the wise men who
attributed immortality to the heavenly bodies—for
this is the point at issue—especially as he intended
it solely for the eyes of a learned friend who would
readily understand his allusion.

I should perhaps say a word on the apparent
contradiction between the division of the speculative
sciences in this tract and that which Boethius gives
in the First Dialogue on Porphyry. There he classi-
fies them as *intellectibilia*, *intelligibilia*, and *naturalia*.[1] How are these to be reconciled with the
theology, mathematics, and physics of our treatise ?
The *intellectualiter* of the tract corresponds, of course,
to the *intellectibilia* of the dialogue, and *rationaliter*
will apply to *naturalia*, but *disciplinaliter* does not
seem at the first blush to have much connection
with *intelligibilia*. I believe the true solution of
the difficulty to be that suggested by Hildebrand,
who sees mathematics included in the class *intelligibilia*. In other words, this *intelligibile* is the
epithet applied to every object of knowledge to be
comprehended by *intelligentia*, as distinguished from
intellectus (the divine instrument of intelligence, which

¹ In Porph. a Vict. trans., Dial. 1, Migne, lxiv. c. 10.

alone can raise us to the contemplation of God), and from *ratio*, which is only capable of comprehending *naturalia* — the objects, that is, of the material world.

Let us now consider what the internal evidence is for attributing the ' De Trinitate ' to Boethius.

In the first place, the division of Difference into the generic, specific, and individual, is exactly the division we find in the translation of the ' Topica ' and in the commentary on the ' Isagoge.'

In this case, not only the thought but the mode of expression is identical. It may be objected that this identity is due to the familiarity of the forger or imitator with Boethius's work. And I am ready to concede that the coincidence, though remarkable, is not convincing. An identity of thought conveyed in different terms would better serve my purpose. But this I find a little later on in the tract, when one of what we may call Boethius's pet theories appears in a form unknown to any of his other writings. It is the contrasting of God's eternity with the perpetuity of the world—a Platonic doctrine which he had made peculiarly his own, and which he intrudes into both the ' Consolation ' and the ' De Trinitate ' at a point where it is not essential to the development of his argument. It cannot, indeed, be said to be out of

place in the 'Consolation,' v. pr. 6, where Boethius
is examining the condition and means of knowledge
of the divine Substance, but it is developed at greater
length than the occasion strictly requires.   But in
the 'De Trinitate,' where his primary object is the
relative in its application to God, he goes out of his
way to treat of the predicaments of time and place.
In both works the thought is referred to the ancient
systems : in the former, Plato's name is given as its
originator ; in the latter, the general expression
secundum philosophos is used.[1]

The 'Consolation' teaches us to say with Plato
that the world possesses life without limit, and must
be called perpetual ; while God embraces at one
glance the fulness of life, and He alone can rightly
be termed eternal.   With Him there is perfect im-
movability, the consequence of an eternal Present.[2]

The 'De Trinitate' gives as the opinion of philosophers that the heavenly bodies are always.   So,
too, is God ; but the word "always" means something very different when applied to Him to what
it does when applied to His creation.   It is, in
fact, hardly appropriate to Him, inasmuch as it suggests a certain change and movement.   The divine

---

[1] See above, p. 122.

[2] "Vitæ immobilis præsentarium statum"—Cons., v. pr. 6.

Now is ever-present, immovable, and so produces eternity.[1]

In view of the exact correspondence of the thought in the tract, " God is eternal, Time is always," with the thought in the philosophical book, " God is eternal, the world is perpetual," we can hardly do otherwise than admit the probability of a common authorship.

To sum up, I am convinced that in the ' De Trinitate ' we possess a genuine work of Boethius— not, indeed, written in the full vigour of his maturity, but before his logical apparatus, so to say, was in working order. Is there any reason to prevent our looking upon it in the light of a learned exercise, suggested, if not imposed on him, by his guardian Symmachus ? I do not see that this view would militate with the MS. title, which, although it speaks of the writer as a patrician, and of consular rank, no doubt ran originally, " Domino Patri Symmacho De Trinitate Boethius." A copyist who knew anything of the life of the famous statesman, and the titles he died possessed of, would be loath to leave his name thus barely stated.

---

[1] " Divinum vero nunc permanens neque movens sese atque consistens æternitatem facit "—De Trin., iv.

II.—Utrum Pater et Filius et Spiritus Sanctus
de Divinitate substantialiter prædicentur.

The treatise ' De Trinitate,' if once established as
authentic, carries with it the two letters addressed
to John the Deacon, whom tradition unhesitatingly
identifies with Pope John, fellow-victim with Boethius to the wrath of Theodoric. A glance at the
synopsis of the MSS. in Appendix A. will at once show
how nearly connected all three writings are. The
variations in the titles of II.—some MSS. announcing
the theme in full, others in an abbreviated form,
while the rest give nothing but the name of him to
whom the letter is addressed—are easily explained.
For in the first place, the motive of the letter is
given in the opening sentence ; and secondly, the
presence of the author's name at the head of the
' De Trinitate ' would be a good excuse for not
repeating it in a work that follows as a sort of
supplement. This argument will apply equally well
to the ' De Hebdomadibus,' which the MSS. are content to introduce with the words, " eiusdem ad
eundem." That the ' Anecdoton Holderi ' vouchsafes no specific information about these two letters
need cause no surprise. " Capita quædam dogmatica "
is a sufficiently exact description of a couple of

treatises, of which the one is too brief and too dependent to deserve a separate notice, while the other
is too metaphysical to be included in a list of religious writings.   For the medieval tradition with
regard   to   them   I   must   refer   the   reader   to
pp. 258 and 259.

The fact that John the Deacon is chosen to grace
the title rather than John the Pope is favourable to
the theory that the tracts were juvenile compositions.
The contention that the copyist must have thought
that the letter " Utrum Pater " (II.) was addressed to
John before his elevation to the pontificate, seems to
me a desperate piece of special pleading.

Nitzsch has the same objections to II. that we
have already heard from him on the subject of I.
He adds, however, to the charge the count of
unwarranted and unacknowledged borrowing from
Augustine.   It is true that our writer says nothing
that Augustine had not already said, and that this
letter is evidently inspired by the ' De Trin.' of the
great African Father.   But this only goes to prove
what I have already suggested, that in matters
theological Boethius was a mere amateur, fond of
trying his hand on difficult questions of dogma, and
anxious to have the opinion thereon of friends more
competent to judge than himself.   It must be ad-

mitted, in passing, that he seems pretty well convinced of the force of his reasoning and conclusions.

The writer is careful not to stray from the lines
laid down by Augustine, and claims for his struc-
ture the foundations of the Catholic faith (" viam
indaginis hinc arbitror esse sumendam unde verum
omnium manifestum constat exordium, id est ab
ipsis Catholicæ Fidei fundamentis ").

No one will deny that Father, Son, and Holy
Ghost, taken separately, are substances; but if we
take them all three together, we get not three substances but one.   This unity of the divine Substance
cannot be split up or divided in any way.   Now it
is not the union of three parts making up a whole,
it is simply one.   Everything that can be affirmed
substantially of the Divinity as a whole may be
affirmed of each of the Persons composing that
Divinity—*e.g.*, the predicate God.   Now this predicate
is a substantial predicate, and so are those others of
truth, justice, incommutability, wisdom, goodness,
power, and all such as can be applied to each of the
Persons separately.   Those predicates, on the other
hand, which can be affirmed of the individual Persons
but not of the collective Divinity, cannot be called
substantial (*e.g.*, the term Father cannot be affirmed
of the Son nor of the Holy Ghost, and so *mutatis*

mutandis). They are rather relative terms, for the
Father must be some one's father, the Son some
one's son, and the Holy Spirit some one's spirit.
Similarly, the Trinity cannot be substantially predicated of the three Persons, for neither Father nor
Son nor Holy Ghost are Trinity, but the Trinity
consists in the diversity of the Persons, the Unity in
the simplicity of the Substance, and a term which
takes its origin from persons cannot be applied to
substance.　　Wherefore Father, Son, Holy Ghost,
Trinity, are terms which can only be affirmed rel-
atively of God.　　All such other attributes as have
been mentioned above can be affirmed substantially
of God.

" I pray you let me know if all this be in keeping
with the Faith ; or if you happen to hold a different
view on any point, consider my words yet closer,
and where you can, make faith join hands with
reason."　　One would think that there was little to
note in such a straightforward statement of a not
very difficult doctrine ; yet it was his commentary
on this tractate (and on the longer letter to Symmachus) that exposed Gilbert de la Porrée to the
charge of heresy brought against him by Bernard of
Clairvaux at the Council of Rheims in 1147.　Gilbert
held that God's essence, divinity, and grandeur were

not God, but the form which made him God; while Bernard maintained the orthodox belief that the divine Essence, Form, Nature, Truth, Divinity, and the like, were God—for if Form were not God, but that which made God, then it would be greater than God.

Bernard praised the orthodoxy of our treatise; and, indeed, though Boethius does not go so far as the French bishop in his identification of the attributes with God, he affirms them substantially of the Divinity.

Gilbert extended to God the same arguments that he was fond of applying to man, that as man is man *quâ* form, so God is God *quâ* form; that the Persons did not make God by themselves, but by the Divinity with which they are identical. But Boethius never tried to assert that the three Persons were not God by themselves, but only that *Trinity cannot be predicated substantially of God.*

III.—Quomodo Substantiæ bonæ sint.

The origin of the second letter to Deacon John was on this wise. John had asked Boethius [1] to explain somewhat more fully (*Postulas ut paullo* . . .

---

[1] It will be noticed that I assume for the moment that this letter was really written by Boethius to John. The question of authenticity will be discussed hereafter.

evidentius monstrem) the essential goodness of substances—a question which had come up in the course
of the "Hebdomades,"[1] and which, from its very
strangeness, demanded a further development. Boethius promises to do his best, and makes excuse for
brevity and obscurity by his wish to avoid the ridi-
cule of the unintelligent multitude. He proposes to
treat the subject on mathematical lines, and accordingly lays down nine preliminary axioms. To save
space, I will only give those ones that are necessary
to a clear comprehension of my analysis of the tract.

"5. Diversum est tantum esse aliquid et esse
aliquid in eo quod est. Illic enim accidens hic
substantia significatur.

---

[1] Hildebrand (*op. cit.*, p. 289, *seqq.*) finds in this word not merely a
reference to the author's classification of his shorter works (as Migne,
ad loc.), but the name of a literary society, of which Boethius, Symmachus, John, and probably Cassiodorus were members, meeting
once a-week to read papers and hold discussions on philosophical
and theological subjects. He regards all the tracts as papers read
before the society, or a further development (as in this case) of questions suggested at its meetings. This interpretation, if it be the
right one, as I am inclined to believe, would justify the writer's
anxiety to keep the results of his learning and research to himself
and his friends, and explains the wilful obscurity of his style ; for a
reader with the discussion of the subject fresh in his mind would
have no difficulty in filling up any gaps in the reasoning. Any way,
it throws a new light on the cultivated society of Rome under Theodoric, and brings us into close sympathy with this little band of
friends who thus laid the foundation of those literary and philosophical societies with which we are so familiar to-day.

" 6. Omne quod est participat eo quod est esse, ut sit.   Alio vero participat, ut aliquid sit : ac per hoc id quod est participat eo quod est esse, ut sit.   Est vero, ut participat alio quolibet.

" 7. Omne simplex esse suum et id quod est unum habet.

" 8. Omni composito aliud est esse, aliud ipsum est."

Armed with these axioms, he begins by-proving that substances are not good by participation nor by essence, and that therefore they are not good at all,—a fallacy which he loses no time in upsetting by the demonstration that they *are* good, not indeed by essence, but by virtue of existence (" in eo quod sunt, bona sunt ").

Proof a. All things make for Good; everything makes for that which it is like ; therefore all things are good.

Now they must be good in one of two ways— either by participation or by substance.   If by participation, then they are not good in themselves, and so they do not make for Good.   If not by participation, they must necessarily be good by substance.   But those things whose substance is good are good in respect of that which they are ; but they owe all that which they are to real Existence

(axiom 5). Their existence, therefore, is good.
But if existence be good, those things which are,
are good in virtue thereof; existence and goodness
are identical terms for them. Substantials, therefore, are good, and being good, they must be like
the supreme Good (axiom 8), and so are that Good
itself, since nothing can be like Good save Good
itself. Hence all things that are, are God, for God
is the supreme Good. "Quod dictu nefas est."
Wherefore substantials are not good; goodness is
not in them, therefore they are not good by right of
existence. Neither are they good by participation,
therefore they are not good in any way.

Proof b. There are many things which, though
they cannot be separated from matter in reality,
can be separated by an effort of the mind and considered abstractly—*e.g.*, the properties of a triangle
can be conceived apart from matter. In imitation
of this mathematical process, let us abstract the
notion of goodness from the supreme Good. Let
us now repeat our first proposition, that all things
that are, are good, and see in what way they could
be good if they had not derived their goodness from
the supreme Good. Now their goodness is not
identical with their existence, for if, for example,
we take a substance which is good, white, heavy,

round, we must admit that each of these qualities springs from a different cause : if each were identical with the substance, then weight would only be another name for colour, colour for goodness, and so on. Then *esse* and *aliquid esse* would be two different things, and substances would be good without in the least degree possessing goodness itself. If, on the other hand, they were none other than Good and had no attributes but goodness, then they would not be things but the causes, or rather the cause, of things ; for goodness pure and simple is the characteristic of the one sole Good. But they are not simple, nor are they independent, but derive their existence from the will of the only Good. Now in the case of the prime Good, goodness and existence are identical ; the secondary Good derives its existence from the prime, the source of the existence of all things. Herein lies the solution of the difficulty ; though things be good in virtue of existence, yet they are not like the prime Good. If their goodness did not come from It, they might be good, but not in virtue of existence. They might, for instance, be good by participation (as a white thing is white, a round thing round, &c.) ; but their existence could not be good unless it were derived from Good. And so, after we have mentally ab-

stracted the prime Good, we see that things which
derive from It may be good, but not in virtue of
existence. Furthermore, since they could not exist
really (as distinguished from abstractly) unless the
true Good had produced them, therefore their existence is good. And unless they had derived from
that Good, though they might be good, yet they
could not be good in virtue of existence, since they
would be *outside* Good, and not *from* it.

Now we need not say that white things are white
in virtue of existence, for they take their being
from the will of God, but not their whiteness—since
He who made them is good, indeed, but not white.
So they are simply white because such was the will
of One who is not white; but those things which
He willed should be good are good in virtue of
existence. It might be thought that on these
grounds all things should be just, since He is just
who willed that they should be. This is not so;
for to be just has reference to an act, to be good
has reference to existence. Existence and action
are indeed identical with Him, but not with us who
are not simple (axioms 7 and 8). Although it is
not possible that with us goodness and existence
should be identical, still it is possible for us to be
good " in eo quod sumus." (So *Proof a* is wrong.)

In a word, all things are good, but all things are not just. Good is a general term, just, a specific ; but species cannot be applied to all things.

Wherefore some things are just, others are something else, but all are good.

Is there anything in the method, temper, or thought of this letter that would warrant our seeking some other source for it than the intercourse of Boethius with his friends ? The mathematical proof is exactly the one which we might expect that he, an acknowledged master in the science, would be likely to employ. That he did employ it sometimes is shown by the following passage in the 'Consolation' (iii. pr. 10) : " I will go a step farther " (it is Philosophy who is speaking on the *summum bonum*), " and following the example of geometricians, who deduce from their preceding demonstrations consequences which they call πορίσματα, I will present thee with a sort of corollary." We meet with the same contempt for the irreverence and frivolity of the common herd, the same proud reserve, the same shrinking from publicity, that characterise the book on the Trinity.

Lastly, one of the principal themes of the 'Consolation,' the striving of all created things after God,

and their derivation from God (iii. pr. 11 and 12),
runs all through the little work before us and receives an almost identical treatment.   A reader who
bears in mind the foregoing analysis will at once see
the intimate connection of its arguments with these
sentences of the ' Consolation ' : " Dost thou allow, or
dost thou not allow, that everything that is good, is
good by participation of Good ?   I allow it " (iii.
pr. 11).

" All things then seek unity ?   They do.   But I
have proved that unity is identical with the highest
Good ?   You have.   All things, then, seek the
highest Good, which may henceforth be defined as
that which all things seek " (iii. pr. 11).

IV.—DE FIDE CATHOLICA.

Before entering upon an examination of the
' Liber contra Eutychen et Nestorium,' I must say
a few words about the ' De Fide Catholica,' which
immediately precedes it in most MSS.   It consists
of a brief survey of Bible history and an exposition
of the great truths of Christianity, such as the doctrines of the Trinity, of the redemption of a lost
and sinful world, of Christ's twofold nature and
single person, of the resurrection of the body,—in

dealing with all of which the heresies of Arius, Pelagius, Mani, Nestorius, and Eutyches are severally refuted. It ends with a statement of the duties and hopes of the Church militant, looking, as it does, for the coming of Christ and a union with Him and with the angelic host on high. A single reading of it is sufficient to convince one that this is no work of Boethius's. Thought, style, and language are all against its authenticity, while the external reasons for its rejection are overwhelming. Up to the ninth century it is unknown, and it is found in MSS. of the tenth, without title and without those glosses with which the other tracts are so plentifully adorned. It was absent from the document which Gilbert de la Porrée employed for his commentary on Boethius, and Abelard makes no mention of it. Indeed, Renatus Vallinus, in the Leyden edition of the 'Consolation' and tracts (1656), is the first to give it the title under which it appears in subsequent editions. Luigi Biraghi adduces for it the evidence of a diptych at Monza. (I describe it from one of the lithographs in Biraghi's book.) [1] This represents a man seated, with toga disarranged and an expression of deep melancholy on his face; his left hand clasps

[1] "Boezio filosofo," &c. *Vide supra*, p. 10.

140

a roll; at his feet, to right and left, are two tablets
inscribed with letters. The writer claims to have
succeeded where Gori[1] and Frisi[2] both acknowledged
themselves defeated, and deciphers the tablets as
bearing the names of the 'Consolation' and a book
against Basilius the informer, each signed with the
name, and setting forth the rank and honours, of our
philosopher. The writing on the roll is declared to
be " In fide Jhesu maneam," and thereon is founded
a long defence of Boethius's martyrdom and the
genuineness of the 'De Fide.' After all that has
been said on the subject, no one will be ready, I
suppose, to reopen his mind to the worn-out belief
that Boethius was a martyr; and even if Biraghi's
conjectures be correct, which cannot be decided
away from the diptych itself, they prove absolutely
nothing with regard to this undoubtedly apoc-
ryphal book. In a twelfth century MS. of the
works of Boethius in the Cambridge University
Library (Dd. 6, 6) this tract is ascribed to *Sancto
Severino*. This may possibly give the key to a solution of the difficulty. There were upwards of a
score of *Sancti Severini* before the seventh century,
of whom one was the famous Apostle of Noricum,
and another, Bishop of Cologne (?) and the author

[1] Thesaurus vet. dipt., ii. p. 248.   [2] Mem. di Monza, vol. iii.

of a *Doctrina De Sapientia*.[1] May it not be this
last—he is at any rate the sort of man—to whom
we should refer the ' De Fide ' ?   A scribe knowing
the name Severinus chiefly in connection with A. M.
Severinus Boethius, the reputed martyr, would easily
have been led into combining the tract in question
with other works of an apparently similar nature.
I have no doubt that on inspection other MSS.
would be found to bear the same title.

V.—LIBER CONTRA EUTYCHEN ET NESTORIUM.

In this, the longest and indubitably the most
interesting of the Boethian tracts, we have a work of
a very different character.   Animated by a certain
religious ardour which we may vainly look for in
the rest, it bears traces of a finer touch and a more
thorough mastery of the subject in hand.   It is,
in a word, quite worthy to take an honourable place
beside the letters of Leo and Cœlestine as a protest
against the heresies which caused the first great
schism between the Western and the Eastern
Church.   Moreover, it betrays a considerable originality of thought and treatment, whereas the treat-

[1] So says Pezius, Anecd. Thes. iv. part 2, p. 1.   See, too, Fabricius,
Bibl. Lat. Med. et Inf. Æt., *s. v.* "Severinus."

ise on the Trinity and the letter to Deacon John are
simply elaborations of Augustine's theme. Here
theology is in no way sacrificed to philosophy, although, as we shall presently see, it is on the development of certain logical sequences that the
value of the work depends. I shall proceed as
usual to analyse the whole before attempting to
consider the method of treatment or the probable
circumstances of its composition.

Introduction.—The writer begins by telling of a
certain stormy assembly at which he was present
when a letter from a bishop combating the heresy
of Eutyches was read and discussed. Interest in
the subject and surprise at the gross ignorance of
most of the audience led him to consider the
question more profoundly, and he now lays the
result of his cogitations before his friend (Deacon
John ?) for his judgment and sanction. His object
has been in the first place to confute the errors of
Eutychianism and Nestorianism, and in the second
to establish the Catholic faith on the nature and
person of Christ. He must begin, however, by de-
fining what he understands by these two terms.

Chapter i.—Nature must be thrice defined to
match the threefold ways in which we are accustomed to employ the word.

1. Nature is the totality of all things, be they substances or accidents, which can be comprehended by man's understanding. But the term must not be restricted to objects perceptible through the medium of the senses. It is applicable to God and to matter as well (by matter the writer undoubtedly means Aristotle's first matter, that which can be discovered by human understanding, not that which discloses itself to pure intellect).

Or, 2. Nature is applicable to substance only. All accidents are thus excluded, and it becomes simply that which can do or suffer. Now Aristotle confines this term to bodily substances only. All accidents are thus excluded from nature, which must accordingly be defined as the principle of movement, acting by itself and not through any intermediary accident.

Or, 3. Nature is the specific difference that clothes any object with its distinguishing form. This last view is tenable if we confine our attention to one thing, whose essential and distinctive peculiarities are summed up in the expression " its nature."

Chapter ii.—Reverting to definition 1, the writer shows that the conception nature embraces a far wider field than the conception person ; for accidents can never be endowed with personality. He next divides substances into the corporeal and the incorporeal, but quickly leaves the former to dwell on the latter, which he subdivides into animate and inanimate beings. Animate, sentient beings are either intelligent or unintelligent. The term person can be applied only to individuals : of all earthly creatures, man is the only one to which it can be applied. In placing God and the angels in the same class with man, as he presently does, he departs from his original premise, which separated corporeal from incorporeal beings.

Chapter iii.—Person now receives a more accurate definition. It is the indivisible substance of a rational, understanding nature. Hence it follows that a person must be both rational and individual. The etymology of the word person next engages his attention, and he takes the opportunity of laying stress on the superior flexibility of Greek as compared with Latin. *Persona* is of course a translation of πρόσωπον, the actor's mask, but the full meaning which we attach to the word is rather to be found in ὑπόστασις. It is always best, he observes, to go back to the Greeks for a clear understanding of such conceptions, for they originated with them, while the Latins only know them through translation. So he proceeds to give the derivation of *essentia* and *subsistentia*,

the one from εἶμι through οὐσία, the other from
οὐσιώομαι through οὐσίωσις. These last terms can
only be applied to universal and generic ideas
whereas ὑπόστασις and *persona* apply to individuals
alone, because nature subsists in them only as a
receiver of accidents.

He ascribes to matter, following the directions of
Aristotle, the potentiality of existence, which potentiality becomes actuality by the agency of form.
Upon it all being depends in order to become a
substance—an individuality.[1] As it would be confusing to bestow the title of ὑπόστασις, *substantia*,
on unintelligent beings, a special term, *essentia*, has
had to be invented to designate the higher forms of
existence.

He next considers the above conceptions in their
relation to God and man. Beginning with man, he
shows that he possesses (1) essence, because he is;
(2) subsistence, because he is not an accident received by another object; (3) substance, because he
is capable of receiving accidents himself; (4) personality, because he is an intelligent individual.

To God, on the other hand, belong (1) essence, for
He is the source of all things; (2) subsistence, for
the same reason that man possesses it; (3), being, for

[1] Cf. De Trin., c. ii.

He is being and a definite being. This last attribute comprises (3) and (4) of man's attributes. Our author's next sentence clears him from the charge of Tritheism, to which his last conclusions might seem to expose him. Substance, he says, in the sense of that which is subject to accidents, cannot be predicated of God, for He is the origin of all things. It is further true that the three hypostases or substances which he attributes to God are not quite in accord with the teaching of the Church. And he himself recognises the difficulty (" nisi tres in Deo substantias ecclesiasticus usus excluderet "), but his object is to show that substance cannot be applied to God in the same sense that it is applied to man, and not to ventilate any heretical opinion.

Chapter iv.—Nestorius held that each of Christ's natures, the human and the divine, demanded a separate personality. The effect of this belief is not merely to divide Christ into two, but even to destroy His identity altogether ; for a distinct name can only be given to that which possesses individual unity. The second consequence of the Nestorian error is the disappearance of all miracle in God becoming man. The human nature in Christ would be due to that want of inner communion with God which is the cause of our humanity ; and the miracle performed by God in Christ's person would be no greater than that which He has often manifested in the persons of the saints, each of whom would thus become a very Christ, not in the metaphorical but in the real sense of the word. The divine and human natures of Christ, if not combined in the unity of a person, must stand further apart than man does from the beast, which both belong to the same natural family of living beings.

The result of such conclusions as these would be the upsetting of the whole fabric of the Christian faith. For Nestorius, by denying that God could clothe Himself in our nature, deprives mankind of the *need* of a redeemer, and God could only redeem that nature which He had taken upon him. And so the Old Testament were all in vain ; and the words of the prophets, which told of the coming of a Christ to save the world, were spoken to no purpose.

Chapter v.—He now gives his closer attention to Eutyches and his monophysitic heresy. Although it was not against Nestorianism that the present treatise was principally directed, the foregoing refutation of that heresy was necessary for a clear understanding of the middle course steered by the Catholic Church between it and the opposite extreme of Eutychianism, with which the author now grapples.

While Nestorius inferred a double personality from
the double nature of Christ, Eutyches believed
that unity of the person involved unity of the
nature. He could not deny the separation of the
divine from the human nature before the union
in the person, but he refused to admit it after that
union had taken place. The precise moment that
he assigns for the union is not certain. Boethius
lays before us two alternative periods,—(a) the moment of generation, or (β) the moment of resurrection — the opening and the closing scene of our
Lord's life on earth. If at the moment of generation, He must have, or not have, derived his earthly
body from the Virgin Mary. If the former hypothesis be the true one, we must suppose a separate
creation, and a mere passage of our Lord's body
through the body of the Virgin. If the moment of
resurrection be given for the effecting of the union,
the difficulty still remains — mankind is still in
Adam's sin and unredeemed, for God could only
have redeemed that nature which He had taken upon
Him. He now returns to a.

Without the aid of the Virgin, man's nature either
must have, or have not, been wholly and completely
undertaken. But to accept the former alternative
would be to disregard all the teaching of the Old

Testament, which derives the Christ from the stock
of Abraham and Jesse ; while by believing the latter,
we should make God a liar. For then were Christ's
body but a deceiving phantom, or something different from our human bodies. To what purpose, then,
the tragedy of His life and passion ? God, as has
been often remarked already, could only redeem
that nature which He had in very truth taken
upon Himself. It is this last conclusion that
Boethius turns against Nestorians and Eutychians
alike, both of which start with a misconception of
the meaning of nature and person.

Chapter vi.—If Christ derived His human body
from the Virgin Mary, then three alternatives present
themselves—

 Either (1), Godhead was changed into manhood ;

  Or (2), manhood was changed into Godhead ;

  Or (3), both natures were so blended that each
   lost its proper essence and gave place to
   some third condition.

Now of these, (1) is impossible and incredible,
and (2) is put out of the question, if we believe that
God took upon Him a human body and soul at the
birth of Christ. For there can be no interchange
between things corporeal and things incorporeal, and
vice versâ. Things corporeal can only interchange

when both possess the same substrate, as water and wine, minerals and plants. Incorporeal bodies have no substrate at all, therefore the human soul cannot be interchanged with the Godhead, nor the body of man converted into the divinity of God.

(3), too, is quite impossible; for while water and honey, for example, can so blend and mingle that each loses its separate identity, it is because these substances possess qualities which can pass into one another, and act on one another; and this does not apply to Godhead and manhood.

Chapter vii.—Having thus crushed both Nestorianism and monophysitism, he proceeds to establish the Catholic doctrine—" Christum in utrisque et ex utrisque naturis consistere."

Christ is not only composed of two natures, but subsists in two distinct natures. The example he adduces in support of this position is that of a crown composed of gold and precious stones, where each factor preserves its separate nature intact; and although they could exist apart, yet *quâ* crown, they have only one existence. The miracle of this communication of the proprieties of the two natures he explains by the single personality acting by the *communicatio idiomatum*. Man suffered, and so did God, inasmuch as He had taken man's nature

upon Him. And so the man Christ is called the
Son of God, not because the human nature passed
into the divine nature, but because the human
nature was united to the divine in one person. One
and the same is perfect God and perfect man—God
of the substance of His Father, and man of the body
of His mother. And so the Catholic faith does
away with the necessity for a fourth hypostate, that
of the human nature. " Fitque in eo gemina natura
geminaque substantia, quoniam homo Deus, unaque
persona, quoniam idem homo et Deus."

He closes this chapter with an enumeration of
four possible combinations of the natures and person
in Christ. These are—

(1) Two natures and two persons—Nestorianism.

(2) One nature and one person—Eutychianism.

(3) Two natures and one person—Catholic faith.

(4) One nature and two persons, which is manifestly absurd.

Chapter viii.—" Quis fuerit status vitæ Christi."
Boethius here deals with the monophysitic conclusion
that Christ must have participated in Adam's sin by
taking upon Him Adam's nature and flesh. The orthodox conclusion is induced by a comparison of three
possible states or conditions of man with regard to sin :

(1) The state of innocence before the Fall ;

(2) A hypothetical state of impeccability, bestowed
     on him by God as the reward of obedience
     to His will—an impeccability precluding
     sin and therefore death ; and

(3) His present state of sin and death.

He shows that Christ has taken unto Himself something from each of these states—from (3) His passion
and death, from (2) His freedom from sin, and from
(1) His subjection to the necessities of the human
body ; and then brings the treatise to a reverent close
with the words of the Lord's prayer, " Thy kingdom
come, Thy will be done.   Deliver us from the evil one."

Epilogue.—As in each of the other theological
writings, he begs for his critic's friendly judgment
and direction if he have strayed from the right path.

Although, as I have already observed, the ' Liber
contra Eutychen et Nestorium ' shows more real religious feeling than the rest of the tracts attributed to
Boethius (with the exception, perhaps, of the spurious
' De Fide '), yet the treatment throughout is mark-
edly philosophical, and, if I may say so, artistic.
The very notion of contrasting the two great heresies
and making them serve as a foil to the orthodox
belief is characteristic of a logician, and hardly one
that would suggest itself to the fifth-century con-
troversialist.   The loving way in which the writer

lingers round the terms " nature " and " person," the
skill with which he demonstrates where and how Eutyches and Nestorius are at fault, the calm statement of his propositions and his reasonable deduc-
tions therefrom, all tend to place this treatise in a
different plane from the ordinary polemics of that
date. We may, I think, fairly refuse to put it later ;
for Nitzsch, who would assign to the composition of
the ' Quomodo Substantiæ ' (I.) an age subsequent to
Boethius, states positively that this book must have
been written about 451, the year of the Council of
Chalcedon,—in the generation, that is, immediately
preceding our author. He says that it is incon-
ceivable that the very shibboleth of the Church party
should have been designated as new and strange
by a writer some fifty years after the Council had
put Nestorianism *hors de combat*, that the doctrines
of the double nature and single person should have
been first brought to his notice by such a letter as
the Introduction describes.

The answer to this objection is the obstinate fact
that between 483 and 518 the question of the
nature of Christ did seriously engage the minds of
Western theologians and that Pope Gelasius himself
(†496) wrote a book upon it.[1]

[1] Usener, *op. cit.*, p. 54.

The date of Boethius's tract is not difficult to fix approximately, the limit in the one direction being the year just mentioned, 518, when the schism was healed and the two Churches reconciled, and in the other the first decade of the sixth century, when our author began his public life.

It has been suggested with great probability that the episcopal letter spoken of in the introduction was the one addressed to Pope Symmachus by the eastern bishops.[1] This letter is dated 512, just two years after the consulship of Boethius and in the very heat of the struggle with Constantinople. There is indeed a curious correspondence between the points it raises and the answers given by the writer of the 'De Persona.' Thus the bishops beg for enlightenment as to the middle way between the diabolical errors of Eutyches and Nestorius which he is at such pains to point out. If the clergy showed hesitation in the matter of Christ's personality, how can we be surprised that a layman should be struck by the novelty of certain expressions connected therewith? " Ex duabus et in duabus naturis Christum consistere,"—this is the burden of the letter, and Boethius dwells at length both on it and on the accompanying question of

[1] Epistola orientalis ad. Symm. ; Mansi, t. viii. p. 222 *seqq.*

the "adunatio." Perhaps we may find in the
bishops' difficulty about Nestorianism Boethius's
reason for dealing with it before engaging with the
great rival heresy, which he tells was the main
object of his attack.

The further objection raised by Nitzsch, that this
letter was the work of several bishops, while the
Introduction to our tract speaks of only one, seems
to me as captious as his other against the *secundum
philosophos* of the 'De Trinitate.' In connection
with this I must mention another passage where
Boethius records his dissent from Aristotle in terms
which at first sight seem less respectful than those
which so devoted a follower of the Stagyrite would
care to utter. " Sicut Aristoteles ceterique et eiusdem et multimodæ philosophiæ sectatores putant,"
he says in the course of his definition of nature (' In
Eutychen,' I.) This definition differs from Aristotle's, in so far as the Greek philosopher restricted
nature to corporeal beings, while the Latin extends
it to God and the angels. But a nearer inspection
shows us that the word in which the sting lies—if
sting there be, for *multimodus* is not necessarily a
word of contempt : cf. Lucr., i. 894 ; Livy, xxi. 8
—does not apply to the master at all, but to the
various schools that claimed descent from him ;

and we know that Boethius, eclectic as he was, had
little patience with views which did not satisfy his
reason.[1]

But even supposing that all I have said on the
probable authenticity of Tracts I., II., and III. be true ;
supposing that in the 'Anecdoton Holderi' we possess
the long-wished-for evidence of a learned contemporary ; supposing that Boethius was the author of
Tractate V.,—and apart from the general contention we have so often heard before, that his other
authenticated writings bear no trace of Christianity,
there is really nothing to prevent us considering
him as such, — there still remains the difficult
problem as to the motives which led to its composition.   What can have induced the statesman and
philosopher, who had hitherto busied himself with
theology only so far as it gave him scope for the
exercise of his logical faculty, to rush with such
ardour into the monophysitic controversy ?   It will
be a great help towards solving the problem if we
bear in mind that the question of the one person of
Christ was, at the time I write of, fraught with an
interest quite as much political as religious.

Ever since 484, the year of the mutual excom-
munication of Acacius and Felix, the see of Rome

---

[1] Cf. Cons., v. pr. 1, where he attacks the Stoics

had been fighting for the primacy with the see of
Constantinople. This estrangement of the pontiffs
could not fail to extend to the political relations of
the two capitals, especially after Odovacar's assertion of his right to control the papal election, which,
even if it were scornfully repudiated after the tyrant
had disappeared, indicates significantly enough how
closely connected were the interests of the bishop
and the ruler of Rome.

And although Theodoric shrank from meddling
in Church disputes—arbitration in the rivalry between the popes Symmachus and Laurentius was
not courted but most unwillingly accepted by him—
yet he was fully aware of this identity of interests, and
saw clearly how essential it was to his own political
supremacy that the Church of Rome should maintain
the ascendancy which was hers by right of apostolic
succession and all the great traditions that still
surrounded her name.[1] Thus there was every inducement for a politician to win the favour of both
his royal master and ghostly father by throwing in
his lot with the Roman Church in her strenuous

[1] I regret that the space and time at my disposal forbid me to go
further into this most interesting question. For a full account of
Odovacar's decree, and Theodoric's dilemma, the reader should go
to Hehle, Conciliengeschichte, Bd. ii. 164, and Hodgkin, *op. cit.*,
vol. iii., chaps. iv. and xi.

endeavour to get Acacius anathematised and the
council of Chalcedon restored to honour; while the
very subtlety of the points at issue would add zest
to the task, if the politician were one who knew his
intellectual superiority over the mass of his contemporaries, whose whole leisure was devoted to
science, and who would be glad to profit by any
opportunity to keep the weapons of his dialectic
free from rust.

Let me not be misunderstood. I would not for
one moment disparage the zeal which marks the
tract before us, or impugn the conviction of its
writer; only it seems to me that he would probably
take a more lively interest in a question that bore
so directly on the liberty of Rome than in those
which exercised his learning and ingenuity, and
nothing more.

Those who believe that Boethius's faith was not
strong enough to bear the ordeal of desertion by his
friends and an unjust condemnation, will doubtless
trace some of his later coolness towards Christianity
to the very fervour of this tract. For if, as I believe, he had the welfare of his city as much at heart
as anything else when he wrote the 'De Persona,'
the mere thought of it, as he lay in prison at Pavia,
must have added poison to the cup of his suffering.

He may be imagined arguing to himself something
after this fashion. " Rome has wrung from Constantinople the confession of her primacy, only to fall a
victim to a tyranny at home which has crushed out
of life the little there was left of her ancient spirit.
Theodoric has only had to let his suspicion be
awakened by the growing intimacy between Justin
and our Church, to let her feel how little he really
cares for orthodoxy or heterodoxy, so long as the
land enjoys peace and justice, and he has the ad-
ministering of both. Of what avail, then, that earnest
attempt to raise the Faith above the mire of heresy?
of what avail that double stroke for old Rome and
the Church? Surely it were better, now that death
is so near, to put away the memory of such wasted
efforts and misdirected energy, and return to the
consolation of her who has never failed me, whose
methods I was wrong to apply to questions both
dangerous to attempt and profitless when mastered.
Come then, Philosophy, be once more my guide and
my teacher! Show me once again how man in his
miserable strivings after partial happiness misses the
whole, the only Good."

CHAPTER VI.

ON SOME ANCIENT TRANSLATIONS OF BOETHIUS'S
LAST WORK.

BOETHIUS wrote long and bitterly on the fickleness
of Fortune, and quoted the stories of Crœsus and
Paulus Æmilius as examples of it. There could be
no better instance given than the way in which
the star of his own renown has paled and set.
From being the favourite author of our ancestors, he
has passed into the limbo of exploded philosophers.
Of ten educated men, you shall not find one to-day
who knows more than his mere name, and perhaps
the title of his great book ; ninety-nine in a hundred
would be unable to give the smallest detail of his
life and work. But if he wins no applause from us
now, he once enjoyed a meed of fame such as falls
to the lot of few writers of antiquity. Of the part
he played in the middle ages as the preserver of

Greek philosophy, and especially of Aristotelianism, I hope to speak in the next chapter. My present object is to trace something of the influence of the 'Consolation of Philosophy'—"that golden volume," as Gibbon calls it—on one side of medieval literature, that of vernacular translation.

The causes of this influence are not far to seek. As I have already said, Boethius stood illumined by the last glories of the old world, ere it sank into what we are pleased to call the darkness of medievalism, and men would bear the vivid impress of that noble figure in their minds long after his masters and teachers, and the sources from which he drew his inspiration, had been allowed to fall into oblivion, not to be revealed before the dawn of the new learning.

Then the subject of his book—steadfastness under stress of misfortune, and the transient nature of all human happiness—is one which is always latent in the thoughtful mind, and only needs the kindling touch of sympathy to start into life; and this, the last utterance of a steadfast race, could not fail to find an echo in the hearts of all those who knew what injustice and misfortune meant. There is, besides, in the 'Consolation of Philosophy' a remarkable medieval note, an anticipation of thought in virtue of which its author is brought as close to Villon, as he is to Cicero and Horace in virtue of style and expression.

" Mais où sont les neiges d'antan ? " sang the vagabond poet of Paris, when he would bring home the lesson that death puts an end even to renown. " Where are the bones of the faithful Fabricius ? where are Brutus and Cato the stern ? " is the form which this sentiment, unknown to classical Latin, takes in the ' Consolation ' (ii. pr. 1).[1] His very anthropomorphism, his realistic personification of Fortune and Philosophy, would commend him to middle-age writers. Is there not, for example, something of their own quaintness in his picture of Philosophy frouncing up the hem of her robe to dry the prisoner's tears ? So strongly does this note assert itself, that I venture to say that any one who has read and re-read the ' Consolation,' and then turns the leaves of some fifteenth-century MS. translation, will find little or nothing anachronistic in the scarlet-and-blue bedhangings, the fur robes and extravagant " hennins," which figure in the miniatures.

[1] It has been pointed out to me that Mr G. A. Simcox has been beforehand with me here (Hist. Lat. Lit., vol. ii. p. 442). I do not think that any one who reads the " Ballade des dames du temps jadis," with Boethius's lines in his head could fail to see the likeness. Still I am very glad to have for my statement the support of so acute a critic.

The springs and influences of literature in the early middle ages were so entirely the same for the whole of Western Europe, that I shall not attempt to hunt down translations of Boethius in any one country before turning to another, but shall for the nonce at any rate treat them as they come in chronological order. But before entering on a search after translations of Boethius, I have a word to say which should not be without interest to all readers and writers of English, on some traces of the 'Consolation' in the poem of ' Beowulf ' (eighth century ?)

SECTION I.—' BEOWULF.'

Authorities.—I have enjoyed the privilege of a sight of Professor Earle's translation, now printing. The text I have used is Heyne's (4th ed., Paderborn, 1879).

This, the earliest and greatest of our secular epics, was probably the work of a North-Anglian, who took for his subject the deeds of the Gothic hero Beowulf, and especially the deliverance of the banquet-hall of Hrothgar, king of the Danes, from the monster Grendel. The limits of my subject forbid me to linger long over this noble poem, with its vigour of picturesque description—now of the start of a warship, bearing forth into the unknown the dead body of a king ; now of the wolf and the raven at work on

a battle-field where dead hands hold out the spear
stiffly against the cold grey of the morning; and with
its swinging verse full of the large air of the northern
seas. But there is one feature in its style which
merits our particular attention, and that is the constant intrusion, in season and out of season, of philosophical and Christian reflections into the midst of
the romantic material. The writer will halt on the
brink of a stirring adventure, or check the full
current of a dramatic episode, to give utterance to
some sententious apophthegm on the government of
the universe or the instability of human affairs. It
has been suggested that such passages are glosses
from a later, probably a monkish, hand; but if, as
we have reason to believe, the poet of Beowulf was
a man of education and culture,[1] nothing is more
likely than that he should have sought to qualify
the pagan element, unavoidable in narratives of
blood and battle, with corrective reflections of a more
elevated character, drawn from his learned studies.
The most remarkable of these passages occurs at the
beginning of what may be called the 17th fit.

[1] Professor Earle, who sees in Beowulf something authoritative,
and possibly even reproof to royal persons, has pitched upon Hige-
berht, Offa's archbishop of Lichfield, as a likely man to have written
the poem, and suggests that it may have been intended for the benefit of that monarch's young son, Egferth. This theory was ex-
pounded in the 'Times' of October 29, 1885.

Beowulf has come to hand-grips with Grendel, and has driven the monster, reft of an arm, to slink back to his native swamps and die. The king has, in a speech of singular beauty and solemnity, given public thanks to God for His great deliverance, and has received the young Goth as his son. He now orders the restoration of Heorot, and proclaims a feast and a giving of gifts to the strangers. " To each one of those who had made the voyage with Beowulf did the captain of warriors give a precious gift at the mead-bench, an old heirloom ; and gave orders to compensate with gold for that (missing) one whom Grendel had atrociously killed, as he would have killed more of them, had not the Providence of God, had not Wyrd, stood in his way ;—and, the courage of that man. The Ancient One ruled then, as he now and always doth, over all persons of human race ; therefore is prudence each-where best, forecast of soul. Much experience of pleasant and of painful must he make, who long here in these struggling days brooks the world." Lines like these sound strange amid the noise and clatter of a banquet ; and of themselves, apart from their position, they are interesting and noteworthy in the highest degree. For a careful scrutiny of them reveals Wyrd, the pagan goddess, the blind unswerving

dispenser of destiny, in strange conjunction with
the Christian's God.   Out of some dozen times that
Wyrd is mentioned in the course of this poem, there
are only three where she appears as dependent on
God.   The most important of these passages we
have just seen; the others occur at lines 2527 and
2815 respectively.   Line 2527 forms part of Beowulf's words to his men on the eve of his last fight.
He has to contend once more with the accursed
race of monsters, but this time it is no fiend in
human guise like Grendel that bids him brace himself for battle, but a fiery worm or dragon, which,
in revenge for the loss of a great treasure it had in
keeping, has spread ruin over the Gothic land.   For
Beowulf, now old in years and honours, has succeeded to the possessions of his kinsman Heardred,
and he must needs defend his inheritance.   So
speaking in boastful words for the last time, he
declares that he will go forth to meet the monster,
and that he will not go back a foot's breadth from
the encounter, but will abide the issue " as Wyrd
allots us, and the governor of every man."

In line 2815 we have the aged warrior's very
last utterance : he has slain the dragon, but not
before it has inflicted a mortal wound on him with
its fiery breath.   In noble words he gives thanks

to God for that He has suffered him to win so much wealth for his Leeds.   Now his last hour is come. Fate has swept away all his kinsmen into eternity, and he must after them.   He invests with his golden collar and coronet the young thane who alone stood beside him in that grim warfare, and so passes to his rest.

In each of these passages we have clear evidence of the pious mind of the poet,—of his wish to paint his hero's life and death as altogether worthy of an ideal knight; in a word, an anticipation of the chivalry that was to be a chief influence for good in the middle ages.   But in neither do we sound a depth of philosophy such as is reached in the first quotation.   This philosophy, of which the key-note is the working of fate with and under God, the compatibility of human prudence with divine providence, can only have been suggested, I venture to think, by the last two books of the ' Consolation,' which are devoted to a consideration of freewill and its connection with God's government of the world.   Moreover, that the poet of the ' Beowulf ' had Boethius in his mind when he wrote these lines is sufficiently proved by the fact that two of them are translations of passages in the ' Consolation,' if not accurate, yet too closely resembling to be a mere coincidence.

Thus " prudence is best, forecast of soul," cannot fail to recall the " rerum exitus prudentia metitur " of ' De Cons.,' ii. pr. i. and " much experience of bitter and of sweet must he have who brooks the world," although, indeed, it is a sentiment which will find utterance in literature as long as there are minds to think and hands to write, seems to owe the form in which it is here presented to the ' Consolation,' ii. pr. 4, where Philosophy exclaims, " Quam multis amaritudinibus humanæ felicitatis dulcedo respersa est ! "

To sum up, these verbal similarities, added to a quite unusual treatment of the problem of freewill, which, although it is here condensed into half-a-dozen lines, is yet almost identical with that adopted by Boethius in the last two books of the ' Consolation,' make up, as I venture to think, a formidable array of evidence in favour of the theory that the philosophical element in ' Beowulf ' is derived from the Latin work.   Moreover, it must be borne in mind how very limited was the number of purely philosophical books at the command of an eighth-century writer.   As I shall presently show, the whole of the ancient Greek library on the subject before the eleventh century begins and ends with a few volumes of Aristotle and the ' Timæus ' of Plato.

In Alcuin's celebrated catalogue of the York collection, which for three centuries was without a
rival at home or on the Continent, the only writers,
besides Boethius, who have any claim to be called
philosophers are Aristotle, Cicero—and his name is
qualified by the epithet *rhetor*—Cassiodorus, and
Lactantius. The name of Seneca, which is noticeably absent from the list, will at once suggest itself
to the student of medieval literature as one likely to
have afforded assistance in treating the question of
Providence. But neither he nor any of these others
had ever made freewill and its compatibility with
divine providence the subject of his speculations in
the same way that Boethius had done. We must
go back to the 'De fato et providentia' of Proclus
for the view of the problem under which it is here
regarded. And it has already been seen (chap. iv.)
how closely the teaching of Boethius resembles that
of the Neoplatonist on this subject. But there is
nothing to suggest that the poet of the Beowulf,
whoever he was, drew his philosophy straight from
the Platonic spring, but rather the reverse, inasmuch
as the phraseology of Boethius retains in his mind
its integrity.

SECTION II.—ALFRED (849-901).

Authority.—I have used Rawlinson's text of Alfred's translation. Oxford, 1698,

First in chronological order after the ' Deeds of Beowulf' comes another Anglo-Saxon work, King Alfred's translation of Boethius's book, which, apart from the immense personal interest attaching to any literary achievement of this great king, commands our closest attention in virtue of the prominent place it holds in the first translating movement of modern Europe. The circumstances of this new literary activity under Alfred offer a singular parallel to the revival of letters in the fifteenth century, after the long silence of the Wars of the Roses. For eighty years and more the land had been in a wild welter of blood and desolation. The last sounds of the long and deadly strife between Mercia and Wessex had hardly died away, when the hoarse war-cry of the Danes began to ring round the coast from Northumberland to Ayr. Christianity, and all the culture and refinement that were tied up with it, had suffered heavily during the fifteen years that preceded the founding of the English kingdom under Egbert; and now the barbarian invaders, that swept the land in a storm of conquest, bade fair to stamp it out altogether.   At the time when Alfred ascended the tottering throne of Anglo-Saxon power, learning was sunk to so low a state that, as he tells us himself, there was scarcely a man throughout the length and breadth of the kingdom who could read Latin. This is not the place to follow him through the details of his long struggle with the Danes, and we must pass quickly on to the moment when he had barely and almost miraculously rescued his nation from perdition, and had at last breathing-space to address his great mind to the problem of reconstruction and education.   For this purpose he summoned to his court a small band of learned men,— Werferth from Mercia, Grimbald from Flanders, John of Saxony, Asser, his biographer, and Plegemund, who rekindled his enthusiasm for classical studies.

It gives additional lustre to the name of Boethius that such a king as Alfred, inquiring after those books which might with most advantage be set within his subjects' reach, should have chosen the 'Consolation' to represent philosophy in the little library he was preparing for their use.   The names of the companion volumes of the selection are a strong testimony to the esteem in which our author was held by the Saxon king and his advisers.

Beda's 'Ecclesiastical History,' the story, told in
unrivalled manner, of English Christianity—in a word
the Church history *par excellence* of the nation;
Orosius's 'Universal History,' whose words were
accepted and reverenced as classical by all students·
through the middle ages down even to Dante, who
does not seem to have known much beyond;
Gregory's 'Pastoral Care' and 'Dialogues,' of which
the former was to serve as a rule of conduct for the
clergy amid the growing needs of a nation newly
awakened to freedom and a higher spiritual and
intellectual life—the latter as an antidote to the
poison spread by the countless coarse stories which
were all the people had to amuse them.   Nor is
this all.   If, as is most probable, Alfred and his
literary movement gave the first centralised force to
the Saxon chronicle, we have further instance of the
capital nature of the selection in which Boethius
figures as the pattern of the philosopher.

    In view of Alfred's literary motive and personal
tastes, the reader of his translations must not look
for any strict adherence to the original.   He ex-
pands and curtails as the spirit moves him.   He
adds a whole chapter on the geography of Germany
to the history of Orosius; he interweaves with the
'Soliloquies' of Augustine many a page from that

precious nd-book, which, alas! has not come down
to us, wherein he was wont to jot down his passing
thoughts and impressions.   But if he left his mark
on the works of Orosius and Beda, it is in his translation of Boethius that Alfred's personality is most
strongly stamped.   The theme was a congenial one.
He, too, had had some taste of changing fortune in
his own life; he, too, had felt the shock of a fall from
high estate; and though he had now won his way
to his throne again, and could look calmly back at
the dangers and vicissitudes he had come through, he
would not for that reason feel the less sympathy
with the Roman patriot whose only crime—no
crime, indeed, in Alfred's eyes—was that he had lent
an ear to the prayers of those who would fain be
delivered from the yoke of a barbarian tyrant.   This
very sympathy, while it blinded his judgment with
regard to Theodoric, whom he is never tired of
abusing, led him to identify himself so entirely with
Boethius, that the latter is often quite lost sight of,
the king taking his place and giving utterance to
sentiments of which the Roman never dreamt.   Thus
in his seventeenth chapter (corresponding to Book
II. prose 7 of the Latin) he takes the opportunity of
setting forth his ideas as to the duties of a monarch,
and of recording his desire so to live that after life

his memory should still shine bright in the good works he had wrought.

That Alfred had from the first no intention of adhering closely to the text before him, either in thought or form, is shown by his changing the original arrangement of five books of alternate verse and prose into forty-two chapters, and by his substituting for the two persons of the dialogue, Wisdom and Reason in place of Philosophy; and now the Mind, now Boethius, now the personal pronoun, in place of the Philosopher. It is impossible to assign an adequate cause for this frequent change of the grammatical subject; when once his mind had taken fire at some suggestion in the text, he seems to have cast aside his cloak of translator, and to have been sublimely careless in whose mouth he placed the lessons of faith and fortitude which were to lead and guide his readers. In his *naïve* and delightful preface, he pleads " the various and manifold occupations which often busied him in mind and body " in excuse for any imperfection of scholarship or obscurity of meaning. His method of dealing with the difficulty and obscurity of the Latin is summary. He finds out the gist of the philosopher's meaning, and proceeds to adapt and weld it to his liking, as he thinks will be most

profitable to the readers of his time, adding here a
homely illustration, there an explanatory note, now
expanding the frequent sentences into a long paraphrase, and now cutting the knot of an abstruse
passage by the simple expedient of omission, and
interpreting the whole by the light of Christian
doctrine.   One would have thought that Boethius's
verse, with its rigid metre and its strict antithesis of
thought and diction, would have offered an almost
insurmountable obstacle to a translator whose genius was rather initiative than obsequious; yet it
is in his renderings of the Latin verses that Alfred
shows most respect for his original.   It is true that
when difficulties begin to gather in the later books,
he steers clear of verse altogether, and that on the
other hand he cannot resist the temptation of making known to his unlearned reader—though it may
cost him a score of lines to do so—the story of
Ulysses or of Orpheus, which the Latin poet is
content to indicate with a well-chosen epithet.   But
for all that, the rendering of the metres may be
pronounced the most successful, as well as the most
accurate, portion of the whole translation.[1]   His

[1] It is debated whether the translation of the metres in allitera-
tive verse ascribed to Alfred, and appended to the Consolation in
Fox's edition, are the work of his hand; but it is proved beyond
debate that the verse translation was founded on the prose.

prose is informed with intensity and fire, and possesses all the vigour and swing of verse.

In a work that is much more of an original composition than a translation, it is wellnigh impossible to point out categorically where and to what extent Alfred deviates from Boethius. His main additions to the original may, however, be roughly classed under three heads—historical (including geographical allusions, which came readily to his pen, fresh from a translation of Orosius), mythological, and Christian. Thus the first chapter is a brief abstract of the story of Boethius, his suffering and death under Theodoric, and that king's various oppressions. Chap. xvi. contains a further allusion to the Amal, supported by a comparison with that other tyrant Nero, together with an explanation of the causes that drove the kings from Rome. The mention of Cicero always calls up a note on his full name and on his title of philosopher.

Theodoric is again chastised in chap. xxiv.; and Nero and Antoninus, two chapters later, feel the full weight of Alfred's indignation.

The geographical allusions call for little comment. Whenever a name such as Ætna or Circe's island occurs, a note is added about its position and distinctive features.

The mythological element, on the other hand, is very prominent and interesting. The Saxon king was not a little proud of his ancient and classical lore, and lets no chance of displaying it go by. The labours of Hercules, the inhospitable habits of Busiris, the monstrous nature of the Hydra, the genealogy of Circe and her treatment of the companions of Ulysses, the story of Orpheus and his journey to the Shades, are all related at considerable length, and show a wide knowledge of Greek mythology. I have already drawn attention to the Christian form in which the translation is cast. The most casual reader of Boethius cannot fail to be struck by the strong theism that breathes through the pages of the ' Consolation,' which only required a few skilful turns and interpretations at the hands of its translator to show forth as a Christian, nay, almost as a dogmatic work. In Alfred's eyes, the city of Truth from which Boethius is exiled becomes the heavenly Jerusalem ; the haven of quiet whither the wise man turns for shelter from the storms of life is Christ. The mention of the fiery lava-flood of Ætna suggests the Deluge ; the universal rule of obedience to the Creator reminds him of one signal exception, the outbreak of the rebellious angels ; the Titans piling Pelion on Ossa to reach to heaven find a parallel in

Nimrod's vain attempt to scale the sky with the Tower of Babel. When Boethius looked out and saw all creation hastening to its fixed goal, and the awards and penalties meted out to those who had done good and to those who had done evil, he turned to the Roman racecourse for a simile. Alfred repeats the illustration, and brings into contrast the race of which St Paul speaks, where "all run, but one receiveth the prize." He dwells with as much delight as Boethius, and at even greater length, on the infinite greatness of God; and over and above the noble invocation with which Philosophy ends her words of comfort, the West Saxon king crowns his work with a prayer to Him that He will keep him ever, through the merits of Mary the Virgin and Michael the Lord's servant, in purity and goodness, in thankfulness to Him, and in obedience to His commands.

SECTION III.—THE PROVENÇAL POEM, 'BOECE'
(*eleventh century*).

Authorities.—Das Altprovenzalische Boëthiuslied, &c. Fr. Hündgen. Oppeln, 1884. M. Paul Meyer has published the text in his 'Receuil d'Anciens Textes Bas-Latins et Provencaux.' Iᵉ partie. Paris, 1874.

We have now to cross the Channel and seek the South of France, where we shall find our author's

influence almost as active and apparent as it is in
our own country.   One of the very earliest monu-
ments of Provençal that has come down to us is
a fragment of a didactic poem on Boethius.   At least,
in the absence of any evidence to the contrary, and
seeing that the two hundred and fifty-seven surviv-
ing lines are devoted to the Roman philosopher and
the lesson of his life, that they certainly are not the
opening lines of the poem but take up the story at
the moment when he was moved to chastise the
wickedness of his time, we are fairly entitled to
assume that the rest dealt with other incidents in
his career, and possibly preserved more of the conver-
sation between the prisoner and his heavenly visitant.
What we have now before us is a mixture, as the
reader, if he has not gathered as much from the foregoing paragraph, will shortly apprehend, of direct
imitation of the ' Consolation ' and a foreign element,
springing either from some other Latin source or from
the author's own imagination.

I have said that we are taken at once into the
middle of the story.   To be strictly accurate, the
first twenty lines, which obviously hang on to some-

This interesting fragment is found in a solitary
MS. of the eleventh century, now in the Public
Library at Orléans.

thing that has gone before, serve as a sort of introduction to the rest. They proclaim the primary object of the poem, which is to hold up Boethius as a model of conduct before the eyes of the careless youth of the day, living in sin and impenitence and utter forgetfulness of God. The writer classes himself among those who " in youth speak foolishly in the folly of their heart," perhaps in order that his words may carry the more weight as coming from one who confesses to like passions with his readers.

Boethius, we are told, would fain correct the unrighteousness of his age ;—" wicked as men were then, they are far more wicked now," adds the stern moralist. His efforts were unavailing, and only brought him to prison and disgrace. Now Boethius was a great lord, and of a noble presence—

  " Donz fo Boecis, corps ag e bo e pros,"—

a philosopher without a peer at Rome.

He was count of this city, and found such favour with the emperor Mallio Torquator that he was raised to the command of the whole realm. But the title he held dearest of all was that of " doctor of wisdom."

Mallio's successor Teiric was an unbeliever, and would have nothing to do with the friends of the true God, and Boethius had no mind to serve an infidel master; nay more, he took upon himself to chastise Teiric in a public speech. The latter in great anger determined to convict the daring speaker of felony, and to this end caused a letter to be written in the name of Boethius, in which he invokes the help of the Greeks, and promises to betray the city to them. To give the forgery every semblance of reality, the tyrant had the messengers to whom he had himself entrusted it, arrested and cast into prison. He then proceeded to incriminate Boethius. The next day on the Capitol, the common court of justice, where the unsuspecting senator and his peers were assembled, the emperor arrived to carry out his base design and make his accusation. Up sprang Boethius, whose conscience was clear of any such treachery, and sought to free himself from the charge. But to no purpose; his friends stood by and saw him cast into prison.

Up to this point the poet has followed, with uncertain step, indeed, and confused intelligence, a life, or rather two separate lives, of Boethius, preserved in numerous MSS., the one of which says: " tempore Deoderici " (there was then some excuse for the strange mutilation of the Ostrogoth's name) " regis insignis auctor Boethius claruit, qui virtute

sua cs in urbe fuit"; the other: "Boetius iste de
familia fuit Torquati Manlii, nobilissimi viri."

Hündgen accounts for the title "Count of Rome"
by supposing that the poet took the *cs* of the first
quotation for an abbreviation of *comes*.　But M.
Paul Meyer reminds me that "comte" is the frequent translation of *consul*, and *vice versâ*.　Thus,
for example, the 'Gesta Consulum Andegavensium'
is the History of the earls of Anjou.

The *familia* of the second quotation, which is
here nothing more nor less than our English
"family," was apparently taken to mean "household"; and as the head of a household in which
so distinguished a man as Boethius was a servant
must himself have been a man of very exalted
rank, he is given a place in the palace of the
Cæsars.

For the rest of the narrative the poet has, in
addition to these Vitæ Boethii, the philosopher's own
words in the 'Consolation,' Book i., pr. 1.　With
these he interweaves, after the manner of his kind,
a mass of pious reflection and Christian allegory,
which are anything but Boethian in character.

Boethius, then, as he lay loaded with chains and
overwhelmed with misery, directed his prayer to
God, the refuge of all sinful men, complaining

(somewhat as the real Boethius does in Cons., i. m. 1)
that although his earliest essays were in the cause
of wisdom, his muse is voiceless : now he cries like
a child all the day long,—" all my inclinations are
turned to weeping." God is his daily hope and
trust ; from God came his honour, his sovereign
position at Rome, of which he availed himself for
the advancement of the wise, and not for God's
glory ; wherefore God has deserted him and suffered
him to lie in prison ; helpless and destitute, he can
do naught else by night or day than sorrowfully
meditate. Then the sad refrain recurs, " All my
inclinations are turned to weeping."

Mindful of his mission as moral instructor, our
Provençal is evidently determined not to let his
feet stray into the paths of exaggeration. Thus
he maintains that " there never was a man, no
matter how much virtue he possessed, who could
embrace the whole of wisdom "; but he qualifies
this discouraging remark with the admission that
Boethius was not at all lacking in wisdom ; indeed
one could hardly meet with a man endowed with
so much of it. Witness his description of time
and nature.

And now the poet takes the first metre of the
Consolation ' and gives it a new application. In the

original, Boethius laments his unhappy fortune and premature decay ; the Provençal gives us very little of Boethius, and a great deal of himself. Among other moralisations of a perfectly general character, which he puts into the philosopher's mouth, there is an elaborate fantasy of his own on the words, " qui cecidit stabili non erat ille gradu." These are, as the reader will remember, the closing line of the elegiacs with which the ' Consolation ' begins, and simply mean that for all his outward show of firmness, Boethius was standing on the brink of ruin even in the days of his greatest prosperity. This is what grows out of it.

" His friends and kinsmen praised him much for his high position, his riches, and his trust in God." Boethius gives them one and all the lie. " For it is not as they said. It is not well with the man who stands on a fragile ladder, which is ready to fall every moment. The man who stands thereon stands not firm. And who is the man who stands on a firm ladder ? The good Christian who believes wholly in God the Father, the Almighty King, and in Jesus, who had such goodwill that He redeemed us humbly with His blood, and in the Holy Ghost, which descends upon good men. Whatever his body may be, It teaches his soul. The good

Christian who stands on such a ladder will never fall into any torment." I have quoted this passage in its entirety, as being the best possible example of the writer's method of interpreting and adapting the Latin to his own purposes. The rest of Boethius's utterances at this point in the poem are in much the same strain. They contain some excellent advice on the advisability of a man's laying up a store of good deeds in his youth, that he may have wherewith to support him in his old age and win his way to heaven ; a warning that grey hairs and infirmity of body do not come from age alone ; and a deal of wise observation on the uncertainty of human riches and the obstinacy of death. One beautiful and striking simile deserves record :—

> "Si cum la nibles cobrel jórn lo be má
> Si cobre avérs lo cor el christia."

> "As the mist covers the daylight at early morn,
> So cover riches the Christian heart."

To Boethius as he lay lamenting there appeared a lady, the daughter of the king " who has great power." We are not told her name, but the mention of the mighty ruler, the peculiar attributes with which she is invested (she has the keys of Paradise, and with them she can admit her friends to bliss), indicate the Christian Sapientia rather than the

pagan Philosophia. To the description of the visitor
as she appears to Boethius in the ' Consolation ' the
Provençal adds several fresh features. The palace
(note the change of locality) is filled with the brightness of her beauty ; you might see for a distance of
forty cities ; the house wherein she enters would
never need a light.

The eyes of superhuman brightness and penetra-
tion which are given to Philosophy in the ' Consolation ' become a glance so keen that no man could
hide before it ; not even they who dwell beyond the
seas could keep their hearts locked from her. In
both descriptions she can make herself great or small
at will ; in both the lady is fair to look upon, but
yet of ancient days. But there is considerable dis-
crepancy in the details of her dress. Boethius speaks
of it as spun of the finest threads, of cunning workmanship, indestructible, a web of Philosophy's own
weaving. The Provençal poet cannot say what the
robe is made of, but only that it is very good and
of very fine material. Yet he goes on to describe it
somewhat closely. Although it was made more than
a thousand years ago by the lady's own hands of a
web of her own weaving, age has not impaired its
value ; one border of it could not be bought for
a thousand pounds of silver. Love and Faith are

the material of which it is woven.   So fair and
white and shining is it, that the beholder's sight is
blinded.

The π and the θ, together with the ladder of lines
connecting them, which are mentioned as adorning
the lower and the upper border of Philosophy's robe,
but about which no explanation is vouchsafed by
Boethius, have their signification fully set forth here,
and an elaborate allegory is evolved out of them.

The π designates the earthly life, the θ the
heavenly law, " de cél la dreita léi."   Thousands of
birds are climbing [1] the steps of the ladder—steps

[1] The fact that the birds are made to use their feet rather than
their wings for mounting to the upper letter called forth an ingenious suggestion from the late Herr C. Hofmann, who supposed that
the translator read *avibus* instead of *quibus* (Sitzungsberichte of
the Munich Academy, 1870, July 2).   The passage in Cons. i.,
pr. 1, runs thus : "Atque in utrasque litteras in scalarum modum
gradus quidam insigniti videbantur quibus ab inferiore ad superius
elementum esset ascensus."   But without attempting to explain the
method of locomotion, I may remind the reader that the bird con-
stantly appears in medieval art as a symbol of the soul, especially
at the moment of death.   At the miracle-plays it was a custom to
let a bird fly when a person died—a crow for the impenitent thief
and a white dove for the penitent one.

In Herrad von Landsberg's Hortus Deliciarum, a beautiful illu-
minated MS. of the twelfth century, evil spirits are represented by
birds.   And in the same work there is a Jacob's ladder whose rungs
are the seven virtues by which man mounts to heaven.   At the foot
of the ladder is the dragon of the pit, ready to catch those who fall
or descend.—(See C. M. Engelhardt's edition of the Hortus.   Stuttgart—Tübingen, 1818.   Plates VIII. and IX.)

not made of gold, but of some substance as good as gold,—" d'aur no sun gés mas mallor no son."

Many of these birds turn back again; but some of them reach the θ, at once assume another colour, and are received with great love by the lady.

Then follows the explanation of the allegory. The steps of the ladder are made of the different virtues—Almsgiving, Faith, Love, Loyalty, Generosity, Happiness, Truth, Chastity, Humility: together with each of these is mentioned the opposing vices against which they are intended to serve as safeguards. Every good man makes his own step—

"quascus bos ōm si fái lo so degra."

The birds which arrive at the θ are the righteous who have expiated their sins, who trust in the Holy Trinity, and set no store on earthly honours. The birds which come down from the ladder are those mortals who have been good in their young days and known wisdom, but with age have grown wicked and perjured themselves. The devil of the pit has them by the heel!

The poet, after remarking that the lady is of great stature for all that she remains seated, goes on to tell how she has in her right hand a book burning with fire, in her left hand a royal sceptre. The fiery book is the justice of God, wherewith unrepented sins are burnt away (a man would do well to make friends early with *her*—she will prove a good mistress); the sceptre is the symbol of corporal justice.

With these words—

> " Zo significa justicia corporal
> de pee "—

the fragment breaks off abruptly. It seems useless to conjecture whether there was much more to follow, or if in the Orléans MS. we possess the major part of the poem. It is, indeed, hardly conceivable that the writer would have been able to turn to account the metaphysics of the later books of the ' Consolation.' However this may be, if the object set forth in the first words of the fragment was all the teacher aimed at, he has sufficiently realised it in the course of these two hundred odd lines.

Before dismissing ' Boëce,' perhaps a word should be said on its metrical construction. For all that it is of Southern workmanship, it displays the salient characteristics of the Northern French epic.

The line consists of ten syllables, bearing the principal accent on the fourth : a cæsura follows immediately on this accent, dividing the whole into two distinct members—*e.g.* :

> " de gran folliá ‖ per folledat [1] parllam."

---

[1] *Or* " per *foll edat* " (propter stultam ætatem).

Section IV.—Notker.

Authorities.—'Die älteste deutsche Litteratur,' Piper (being the first volume of Kürschner's 'Deutsche National-Litteratur'). Berlin and Stuttgart. The same writer's edition of Notker's works, Bd. viii. of the Germanischer Bücherschatz. Freiburg and Tübingen, 1889.

Of equal importance, from a philological standpoint, is the old High-German version from the pen of Notker of St Gall. Here again we see the place that Boethius holds in the dawning literature of medieval Europe—a place which no other secular writer of antiquity can dispute with him. The reader of the foregoing pages will know something of the help given by the 'Consolation' in shaping the infant utterance of a great Romance language. Its influence on the grammar and phonetics of the *lingua theotisca* is no less remarkable. But this influence, interesting though it be, stands outside the scheme of the present chapter, and I cannot devote more than a few passing words to it, or treat it otherwise than as subservient to the general literary interest of the work before us.

And first with regard to the translator himself. He may be distinguished from his homonyms in the great Swiss monastery in any one of three ways:

by order of succession (he is Notker III., Notkers I. and II. being respectively the sequence-writer, and the doctor and hymnologist); by the personal defect which earned him the sobriquet of *Labeo*, " thick lips " (*they* were nicknamed, the one *Bal-bubus*, " the stammerer," the other *Piperis gramma*, " Peppercorn," from his fiery temper); or lastly— and this is the title by which we would rather know him—by the epithet *Teutonicus*, " the German," given him in virtue of his efforts on behalf of his mother-tongue, and of his position as the initiator of a great school of German translation.

He was born about 950, and died in 1022 of the plague which Henry II.'s army brought back with it from Italy after the campaign against the Greeks of the South. Introduced into the monastery by his uncle, the learned Ekkehart I., he presently rose to be director of the school there—one of the largest and most important in all Europe, which had been in existence long before the revival of letters under Charles the Great. He seems to have been a man of considerable personal charm: his pupil, Ekkehart IV., speaks of him with the warmest love and admiration; and his intellectual range and power may be gathered from the account of the writings, chiefly commentaries and translations, which occupied the leisure of his long and useful life.

These include, on his own showing in a letter to Hugo II., bishop of Sitten, Cato's ' De Moribus,' Virgil's ' Bucolics,' the ' Andrias ' of Terence, Marcianus Capella, Aristotle's ' Categories ' and ' De Interpretatione,' treatises on rhetoric and arithmetic, a psalter, part of the book of Job, Boethius's tract on the Trinity, and the ' Consolation of Philosophy.'

It is probable that all of these books were not written by Notker himself; it is almost certain that he only completed two books of the ' Consolation.' But if he did not actually do all the work, he at least inspired the workers, who carried out his intention so completely as to render it often impossible to distinguish the master's hand from that of the apprentice.

The translation which here concerns us opens with a short and fairly accurate sketch in German of the state of things at Rome in the days of Boethius :—

" St Paul promised those who in his time were awaiting the Last Day that it would not come before the Roman empire had fallen, and Antichrist begun his reign." The author then touches lightly on the rules of Otacher and Thioterih, and on the wresting of the latter's kingdom from him by Alderich, which marks the overthrow of Roman liberty. "When the Goths were driven out under Justinus Minor, there came the Langobards from the north and ruled Italy for over two hundred years. After them the Franks, whom we call Carlings, and after them the Saxons. So now is the Roman empire destroyed, according to the words of the holy apostle Paul."

With this prelude Notker proceeds at once to the " Conquestio Boetii de instabilitate fortunæ."

His method of translation is to give a sentence or group of words of the original (which he arranges for the sake of his pupils in as simple and straightforward a form as possible), followed by the German equivalent. This last is expanded, as the occasion seems to require it, by passages of explanation and paraphrase of varying length. One of the most remarkable features of his style is the way in which he has recourse to Latin to help him out of a difficulty with a turn of expression or a technical term which cannot be supplied from the German. For instance—

1. " Ecce laceræ camenæ dictant mihi scribenda " (the real order of the Latin being, " Ecce mihi laceræ dictant scribenda camenæ ") he renders by, " Tîe "

(*i.e.*, the Muses) " míh êr lêrton [1] ioconda carmina, tîe lêrent míh nû flebilia."

2. " Sed abite potius sirenes . . . " " sirenes sínt méretîer,[2] fóne déro sánge intslâfent [3] tîe uérigen,[4] et patiuntur naufragium."

Each section of prose or verse (I am here speaking of the original divisions of the book—Notker, of course, makes no attempt at a metrical version) has its appropriate Latin heading (*vide supra*).

One can hardly resist the temptation of comparing Notker's ' Boethius ' with Alfred's ; but it is obvious that, apart from their common characteristic of vernacular translation, there is no analogy between them. Alfred's primary aim was to place in the hands of his subjects a volume of philosophy from which he had himself derived help and comfort, and the result is a work of high artistic merit. Notker's object was to teach his scholars Latin through the medium of a book which, besides its intrinsic philosophical value, would readily lend itself to commentary and exegesis, and which was especially useful as an example of close logical argument : the result is a work of unsurpassed philological interest to modern scholars. This is not, indeed, what its

---

[1] Lernten.   [2] Sea creatures (*animal maris*).
[3] Fall asleep (*entschlafen*).   [4] Mariners ferrymen (*Fährmann*).

author intended, but quite what we might have expected; for, as Piper says, Notker's method would
only enlarge the learner's Latin vocabulary, and not
at all impart to him the sound grammatical knowledge which is the basis of all education through
language.[1]   But while the German translation ranks
far below the Anglo-Saxon as literature, it is not
without a charm of its own, and is an admirable
specimen of medieval annotation, with all its fine
careless display of curious knowledge, and its
delightful *naïveté* of illustration.   Let me give a
single example.   When Boethius is describing the
appearance of Philosophy as she stands by his bedside, he says : " Staturæ discretionis ambiguæ (fuit).
Nam nunc quidem ad communem sese hominum
mensuram cohibebat, nunc vero pulsare cœlum
summi verticis cacumine videbatur."

The translation runs as follows : " She was in
her height of doubtful size ; I could not rightly tell
how tall she was.   For now she came down to our
measure (in that she sometimes considers human
affairs), and anon she seemed to touch the sky with
her uplifted head (in that she understands astronomy)."

I have said that Notker's main object was to
teach his pupils Latin.   He had, however, when

[1] *Op. cit.*, p. 353.

he undertook this and kindred translations, another
end in view beyond the mere editing of classical
reading-books for his monastery's school, and one
that touches us far more closely. He was fully
aware of the virtue of the vernacular as a medium
of education, and determined to carry to completion
the scheme of which the outline had been drawn
by Charles the Great two hundred years before
("inchoavit et grammaticam patrii sermonis," writes
Einhart, the biographer of the Frankish emperor);
in other words, he resolved to reduce to order and
fix on a scientific footing the laws of accent and
pronunciation which his countrymen unconsciously
obeyed in speaking their own language. Hrabanus
Maurus (776-856) had already been at work in the
same direction, and had authorised the use of the
circumflex and acute accents to designate long and
short syllables. But it is to Notker, and especially
to his 'Boethius,' that we must turn for our knowledge
of Old High-German phonetics, of the exact quantity
of its terminations and the value of its vowels.

In his letter to the bishop of Sitten he says:
"Oportet enim scire quia verba theutonica sine
accentu scribenda non sunt præter articulos, ipsi
soli sine accentu pronuntiantur acuto vel circum-
flexo." And his practice in no way falls behind

his theory. We can appreciate, thanks to him, the difference between the diphthongs *úi, óu, éi, éu,* and *úo, íe, íu, ío;* between the vowels *i* and *u,* and the consonants *j* and *v.*

The change of *d* into *t, b* into *p,* &c. (in technical language, of initial voiced stop-consonants into voice-less consonants), is carefully recorded, as the follow-ing passage shows : " Sanctus paulus kehîez tîen dîe in sînên zîten uuândon des sûonetagen . táz er êr nechâme . êr romanum imperium zegîenge . únde antichristus rîcheson begóndi . Uuér zuîuelôt ro-manos íu uuésen állero rîcho hêrren   únde íro geu-uált kán ze énde dero uuérlte ? "[1]

In a word, as Dr G. Eduard Sievers points out, he did for German phonetics, only even more fully, what Ormin did for those of England.[2]

The plan I had before me at the beginning of this chapter of dealing with the medieval transla-tions in chronological order without having regard to the countries where they were made, has served well enough so far. But with the eleventh and twelfth centuries there comes a change over Euro-pean literature. The stream which we have hitherto been content to regard as one, breaks up into a

[1] *Vide supra,* p. 192.
[2] Encycl. Brit., *sub voce* " Germany (Language)."

number of branches, which run further and further
apart as time goes on.   France and England, Italy
and Germany, have from henceforward each a literature of their own, and each demands a separate consideration.   The two last, under this new arrangement, will be found to be of small account; and
England must now yield the precedence to France,
for French, both in virtue of the number and the
date of its translations, has the foremost claim on
our notice.

FRANCE.

SECTION V.—SIMUN DE FRAISNE'S 'ROMAN DE FORTUNE' (thirteenth century).

Authorities.—M. Paul Meyer, as recorded in a note. 'Hist. Litt.
de la France,' t. xviii.   Thomas Wright, Biogr. Brit. Lit., ii.   MS.
in B. M., Roy., 20. B. xiv., f. 68* (xiiith cent.) [1]

The earliest vernacular version of 'Boethius,' after
Alfred's, that I have come upon in any language is
the Anglo-Norman 'Roman de Fortune' of Simun de
Fraisne.   With regard to the literature of which it
is an example, M. Paul Meyer has well said [2] that,
however slight its intrinsic merit may be, it deserves

------

[1] I have marked with an asterisk those MSS. from which my
quotations are taken.

[2] 'Bulletin de la Soc. des anciens, textes fr.,' 1880, No. 2.

a close attention, as representing the sustained effort which enabled the language and ideas of France to hold their own for so long on British soil.

But over and above the general interest of this literature, the present example possesses not a little of the genuine poetic instinct.

Our knowledge of its author, Simun de Fraisne (whose name appears in the initial letters of the first fourteen lines), may be summed up in a very few words. He was canon of Hereford, and the near friend of Giraldus Cambrensis. Indeed it is the date of Gerald's death, 1223, that gives us the clue to the period of Simun's literary activity. Besides a number of Latin poems, among them one in defence of the bishop-designate of St David's, he wrote a ' Vie de St Georges ' and the ' Roman de Fortune.' This last is a reminiscence of Boethius, a variation on the description of Fortune in the early books of the ' De Consolatione.' It runs to sixteen hundred lines of eight-syllabled rhyming couplets, and is couched in the form of a dialogue between ' le clerc ' and ' dame Philosophie,' who has the same part to play here that is assigned to her by Boethius, her business being to show the emptiness of earthly riches, honours, and delights. The poem is found in two manuscripts—the one in the British Museum

(as recorded above); the other, and apparently the
more correct, in the Bodleian (Douce MSS. 210).
Of these I have only been able to examine the first,
and that under pressure of time; still I have seen
enough to convince me that there is some ground
for M. de la Rue's eulogistic notice in the 'Histoire
Littéraire de la France.'[1]

I will quote but one passage to show that the
poet had a true feeling for nature—

> " Homme poet auer grant delites
> Quant il veit en mai les flurs
> Esemblant de veus plusurs
> Quant il veit gardins florir
> Ky frut deit le cors norir
> Et veit ben leuer les pres
> Et les champs revestuz de bles
> Ses oils poet de joie pestre
> Pur les bens ky il veit crestre."

Section VI.—Anonymous Writer (*thirteenth century*) and Jehan de Meun (1297-1305).

Authorities.— M. Léopold Delisle, ' Inventaire des Manuscrits,' t.
ii. M. Paul Meyer in ' Romania,' t. ii., 1873. MSS. in B. M.
Add. 21,602 (early xv.); Add. 10,341 (xv.) Harl. 4335-9* (xv.)
Harl. 4330 (late xv.)

Whatever may be our opinion of the character
and aims of Philippe-le-Bel, Dante's

> " Mala planta
> Che la terra cristiana tutta aduggia,"[2]

---

[1] *Loc. cit.*, p. 822.   [2] Purgat., canto xx. l. 43.

we cannot deny his statecraft and his skill in matters of finance. That he was also a friend to learning and letters is shown by the flourishing state of the
University—there were more colleges founded under
this king than during the whole thirteenth century
—and by the numerous literary achievements of his
reign. It was for his edification that Gilles de
Rome, archbishop of Bourges, wrote his treatise,
' De Regimine Principum,' on the model of Aristotle's ' Politics '; it was to his command that Jehan
de Meun translated the ' Rei Militaris Instituta ' of
Vegetius, the ' Merveilles d'Irlande ' of Giraud de
Barri, Abelard's ' Letters,' Ealred's ' De Spiritali
Amicitia,' and the ' Consolation of Philosophy.' This
last he dedicated and presented to the king with his
own hands, if we may believe the miniature which
appears on the first page of many manuscripts.

The prologue contains a courtly compliment to
his royal master on his scholarship (" ja soit ce que
tu entendes bien le latin," &c.), a lengthy disquisi-
tion on the goal which mankind should make for,
and on the profit to be drawn from the pages of the
' De Consolatione ' (" entre tous les livres qui oncques
furent faiz cestui est souverain a despire les biens
vilz et descevables "), a sketch of Boethius's life, and
an explanation of his book.

So far so good. But now comes the difficult
question, which is Jehan de Meun's translation ?
For there are two, entirely distinct, to which this
prologue is affixed. The one is in prose, a word-for-
word rendering : of this there are five manuscripts
at Paris—the oldest, a fragment, dating from the end
of the thirteenth or the beginning of the fourteenth
century. The other, a more scholarly performance,
follows the scheme of the Latin original : of this
there exists an infinity of manuscripts, both in Paris
and London, besides several printed examples. M.
Paul Meyer cannot allow the former to be J. de
Meun's work at all ;[1] but he offers no explanation
of the dedicatory preface. M. Delisle, while he recognises the justness of M. Meyer's remarks, still
speaks of the first as a " traduction en prose, par
J. de Meun," and of the second as a " traduction
en vers et en prose attribuée à J. de Meun."[2]
And there the matter must rest. Whoever was the
author of the first translation (which for the future
I shall style MS. 1097, from the earliest complete
copy in the Bibliothèque Nationale), there is an interesting point about it in connection with Chaucer,
which has as good a right to be considered here as
later.

[1] *Op. cit.*, p. 272.   [2] *Op. cit.*, p. 318.

Dr R. Morris, in his edition of Chaucer's ' Boëce '[1] (p. xiii.), has the following remarks : " Chaucer did not English Boethius second-hand through any early French version, as some have supposed, but made his translation with the Latin original before him. Jean de Méung's version—the only early French translation, perhaps, accessible to Chaucer—is not always literal, while the present translation is seldom free or periphrastic, but conforms closely to the Latin, and is at times awkwardly literal. A few passages, taken at haphazard, will make this sufficiently clear."

Unfortunately, Dr Morris's passages are not taken from any translation by Jehan de Meun. What they are taken from is an anonymous version made in 1477 " par un pauvre clerc désolé quérant sa consolation en la traduction de cestui livre." This was published by Colard Mansion in the same year, and may possibly have been written by the famous printer himself.[2] A reprint of it was issued by Antoine Vérart in 1494, of which there is more than one copy in the British Museum, where it stands catalogued under the name of " Jean de Méung." Hence, I presume, Dr Morris's mistake.

---

[1] E.E.T.S., 1868. Reprinted 1889.
[2] See Gustave Brunet, La France Litt. au XVᵉ Siècle, p. 29.

Now the translation which we may safely look
upon as Jehan de Meun's has evidently no connection
with Chaucer. Half-a-dozen parallel passages will
suffice to show that. But I am by no means so
certain about the other.

Through the kindness of M. Louis Denise, of the
Bibliothèque Nationale, I am enabled to set side by
side with eight out of the twenty-eight passages
selected by Dr Morris the corresponding renderings
of MS. fr. 1097 in the Paris Library.

In the third column will be found some half-
dozen passages which I claim are sufficient to
establish Chaucer's independence of J. de Meun's
translation, at any rate.

CHAUCER.	MS. FR. 1097.	J. DE MEUN.
And sorou haþ com-aunded his age to be in me.	Et douleur a com-mende que les aages me soit venuz.	Tant ay je au mains de compagnie En ceste dolereuse vie.
Þilke deeþe of men is welful þat' ne comeþ not in ȝeres þat ben swete (i. mirie), but comeþ to wreeches often yclepid.	Beneure est la mort des hommes qui ne sembat pas es doulz ans ains vient aus dolereus apelee sou-vent.	Len devroit bien priser la mort Qui homme qui a son confort Ne surprent ne tolt sa liesse Mais quant il vient en sa tristece, &c.
Wepli compleynte.		Ma complainte plaine de pleur.
Wiþ office of poyntel.		(Je) metoie par escript.
Swiche . . . þat it ne myȝte not be emptid.		De trop grand vigueur.
Comune strumpetis of siche a place þat men clepen þe theatre.	Ces communes puter-eles.	Ses vilz ribauldes.

CHAUCER.	MS. FR. 1097.	J. DE MEUN.
Neyþer ouer-oolde ne vnsolempne.	Dont la memoire nest pas moult ancienne ne non moult cele-brable.	
Among my secre rest-ing whiles.	Entre nos oiseus se-crets.	
Þe houndys of þe pa-lays.	Chien du pales.	
Of þi masculyn chil-dren.	De ces deuz enfans malles.	
It deliteþ me to comen now to þe singuler vphepyng of þi wile-fulnesse.	Me delite en venir en sengle comblement de ta beneurte.	
Emperie of consulers.		*Lempire consulaire.*[1]
In þe cloos. Of þilke litel habitacle.		En ce meisme propris de cest brief habi-tacle.
Þe brode shewyng con-treys *of þe heuen, and upon þe streite sete of þis erthe.*		Regart les contrees du ciel larges et grans et lestroit sieges de terres.
Al þouȝ þat þe pleiyng busines of men ȝeueþ hem honiede drinkes and large metes wiþ swete studie.		Ja soit ce que li homme li doingnent par jeu breuvages emmielles et larges viandes par doulz estude.

The reader is now in possession of a certain number of the passages in question. It would not, I suppose, take much more time and trouble to complete the tale. But this method of random selection, though it may serve well enough in the case of works of manifestly different scope and character, such as are Chaucer's 'Boëce' and Jehan de Meun's translation, is a poor

---

[1] M. Denise has sometimes gone beyond the letter of my request, and given me more of the French than I asked for. I am glad of the excuse to supply the English context (in italics) to match the surplusage.

and unsatisfactory test when we have to try two versions which have so many points of resemblance as ' Boëce ' and MS. 1097. Nothing short of a thoroughgoing and systematic comparison of them could make an opinion on the subject worth having, and so I do not propose to offer one. I am only anxious that when excerpts are made from " the only early French version, perhaps, accessible to Chaucer," we should at least be sure that we have the right version before us.[1] When its turn comes, I shall pass Chaucer's work under review, and endeavour to show that it bears, on the face of it, strong evidence in favour of originality.

SECTION VII.—PIERRE DE PARIS (*thirteenth or early fourteenth century*).

Authority. — M. Ernest Langlois in 'Notices et Extraits des Manuscrits,' t. xxxiii., 2ᵉ partie, 1889.

The Vatican Library possesses (Vat. 4788) a prose version and commentary of the ' Consolation,' dated 1309, which we owe to a certain Pierre de Paris, the author of two other unknown translations. M. Langlois in his account of the MS. declares that

[1] As a matter of fact, there is nothing in the mere date of the version either of J. de Cis or R. de Louhans which would put them out of our English poet's reach.

however it may be with the Latin original, the translation often stands in need of commentary.[1]   The
work is preceded by a long prologue in which Pierre
explains his method of work ("je prendrai la lettre
mot a mot, droytement, sans rien changer, et puis si
la exponeray clerement," &c.), and then gives us the
benefit of a study on 'Boethius.'

The translation of i. m. 1 begins as follows : " Je,
Boece, qui ay fait ancienement les dities en l'estude
florissant, hay las ! je, plorable, sui contraint assenler
les vertus tristes."

After an explanation three times as long as the
translation, he goes on again : " Blessay les sciences
depeciees qu'il me ditent choses de escrire, et les
vers de la chaitivité si arosent mes balievers[2] de
verais plors."

At the end the author submits his work to his
patron, some high personage, perhaps the king, beg-
ging his indulgence and intelligent interpretation :
" Je sui certain que tante est vostre debonaireté que
vos suplerois toutes mes defautes et que par vostre
entendement l'euvre sera dou tout clere a tous ceaus
qui vodront avoir la conoissance."

[1] *Op. cit.*, p. 262.
[2] *Bas-lièvres—i.e.*, the lower part of the cheek.

SECTION VIII.—ANONYMOUS POET (138– ?).

Authorities.—M. Delisle, as before ; M. E. Langlois, in 'Catalogue général des MSS. des Départements,' t. vii. ; MSS. in B. M. Add. 26,767 (early xv.), Roy. 20. a, xix.* (xv.)

Certainly during Chaucer's lifetime, and most probably almost synchronous with his 'Boëce,' there appeared in France a translation which is generally known by the words of its first line—

> "Celui qui bien bat les boissons
> [Est dignes d'avoir les moissons]."

Until 1873 it was accepted, on the authority of Buchon,[1] as the work of the famous Charles d'Orléans ; but in that year M. Léopold Delisle[2] proved beyond the shadow of doubt that the conjecture, however ingenious, was wrong, which ascribed this version to the prisoner of Agincourt. Buchon was led to it by a passage in the prologue, where the poet gives as 'the motive of his work a wish to calm the grief caused to a king Charles, who had quite lately mounted the throne, by the misfortunes of his subjects.

I have written it, he says—

> "afin
> Que Charles roy qui a este
> Souef nourri nomme daulphin,

---

[1] Choix d'ouvrages mystiques, tome 21-23 (in the Panthéon littéraire).   [2] *Op. cit.*, p. 317.

> En sa nouvelle mageste
> Ne soit a courroux trop enclin
> Quant voit son peuple moleste
> De la baniere anticristin."

Buchon at once jumped at the conclusion that the young king was Charles VII. and the writer Charles d'Orléans, and proceeded to support his theory by the following arguments :—

1. Charles d'Orléans was something of a Latin scholar, and as such, likely to pride himself on his knowledge, rare in a man of his rank.

2. The handwriting of the Paris and Brussels MSS. is the handwriting of Charles d'Orléans's day.

3. The Brussels MS. has a princely look.

4. The royal personage of the prologue is addressed in terms of familiarity which would be unseemly in the mouth of other than one of his own family.

5. The style and feeling of the translation are in perfect harmony with the style and feeling of Charles d'Orléans's authentic poems.

The date he proposed to assign it was the moment of Charles VII.'s accession—*i.e.*, 1422.

To upset this ingenious fabric a single MS. of date anterior to 1422 is sufficient.   Such a MS. exists in No. 14,459 of the Fonds français in the

Bibl. Nat., written in 1413. (There is one in Trinity Hall Library of 1406.) But M. Delisle's sagacity has enabled him to adduce a yet stronger proof.

To No. 1982 (Fonds fr. nouv. acq.) there is appended an epilogue which gives us the writer's name, Raoul d'Orléans. Now Raoul d'Orléans is perfectly well known as a copyist whose period of activity ranged between 1367 and 1396, and Charles d'Orleans was not born till 1391!

With these facts before us, it only remains to be seen what were the changes from dauphin to king in the latter part of the fourteenth century; and these were in 1364 and 1380, when Charles V. and Charles VI. respectively began to reign.

It is to the last of these years that we must in all probability assign the composition of " Celui qui bien bat les boissons."

Were it not for the mere pleasure of telling the story of M. Delisle's skill and judgment, and how he timely saved French literary history from a serious blunder, I need not have gone so minutely into the details of the case. For at Toulouse there has been found another manuscript of this translation, having an entirely unknown epilogue in thirty-two lines, which tells us by an amusing if somewhat

exasperating periphrasis that the poet was a native
of Picardy, a monk of the order of St Benedict, that
he had been Prior in Savoy, and further, that he
had sat at the table of Louis II. of Bourbon, count
of Clermont in Beauvaisis.   As this nobleman became count of Ferez in 1382, we can have no
difficulty in assigning an approximate date to his
' commensal.' [1]

Here, as elsewhere, I shall give part of the rendering of ii. m. 5 as a sample of the translator's style :—

> " Hee dieux come de grant excellence
> Fu le premier temps dinnocence
> Chascun des biens contens estoit
> Que Nature lors lui donnoit
> Point ne se vouloient dilater
> Ne de lieu en lieu translater.
> .   .   .   .
> Quant jeune le jour auoient
> Au vespre glans sans plus mangerent
> Ilz ne sauoient questoit vin
> Point ne cuilloient le raisin
> Lors nestoit point les artifices
> De clare de miel et despices.
> .   .   .   .
> Encor nauoit sonne trompete
> Qui les gens darmes ammoneste
> Ne sang par cruelles haynes
> Nauoit fait les armes sanguines.
> .   .   .   .   .   .

---

[1] Langlois, *Op. cit.*, p. 470.

> Laz cum de male heure nez fu
> (Cil) . . . qui par sa feruant auarice
> Tant foux que par artifice
> Celle chose qui veult celer
> Nature ce fist reueler
> Et terre tant parfont affine
> Que cuers humains art et mine."

There is a third version in a solitary MS., dated 1397, which M. Paul Meyer declares to be but "un vulgaire plagiat" of J. de Meun's translation.[1]

Section IX.—Jehan de Cis (*fourteenth century*).

Authority.—M. Paulin Paris, 'Les Manuscrits français,' t. v., 1842.

The Bibl. Nat. possesses yet another fourteenth-century rendering, coming from the hand of a fellow-townsman of Jehan de Meun. This common birthplace naturally led to a confusion of the two writers, and indeed the copyist of MSS. fr., No. 576 (fifteenth century) assigns it to the poet of 'Le Roman de la Rose.' But M. Paulin Paris in 1842 finally dispelled this illusion, and conjectured the author to be Jehan de Cis, a Dominican,[2] of whom mention is made in the epilogue of the translation beginning "Celui qui bien bat les buissons."

The obscurity and affectation of the work we are

[1] Romania, 1873, p. 272.   [2] Les MSS. fr., v. pp. 46 and 52.

considering are sufficient excuse for a fresh translation such as the one which used to be attributed to Charles d'Orléans.

Section X.—Frere Renaut de Louhans.

Authority.—M. Paul Meyer in 'Romania,' t. ii., 1873, p. 272. MSS. in B. M., Roy. 19. a, iv.* (early xv.); Eg. 2633 (xv.)

Passing over a prose translation into French by an Italian (fourteenth century) and a verse translation which M. Meyer has shown to be nothing more than a variation of "Celui qui bien bat les buissons,"[1] another verse translation must be remarked, which enjoyed a great vogue, to judge by the number of MSS. extant.   Its date is fixed by the words of the epilogue as 1336, and the author's name, Frere Renaut de Louhans, is given by the initial letters of the nineteen octaves of the prologue.

Frere Renaut appears to have paraphrased rather than translated the 'Consolation.'   Thus, in dealing with ii. m. 5, he is not content, like Boethius, to contrast the former with the present age, but divides the life of the world into four periods—the first, of innocence; the second and third, when agriculture and avarice respectively began; the last, our own, "plus mauvais que les quatre devant."

[1] *Op. cit.*, p. 272.

I will quote a few lines as a specimen of his closer adhesion to the Latin :—

> " Nestoient perduz par outrage,
>   La glan mengoient du boscage
>   Quant jeune grant piece avoient
>   Clare ne pyment ne buvoient
>   Et ne savoient artifices
>   Comment le vin et les espices
>   Se doivent ensemble meller
>   Dieu ne leur vouloit reveler
>   Comment li drap se coulouroient
>   Tout vestu sur lerbe gisoient
>
>   .   .   .   .   .   .
>
>   Ilz buvoient a grant alaine
>   Leaue qui vint de la fontaine
>   Car ne cognoissoient les vins.
>   Sur les arbres et sur les pins
>   Estoit leur habitacion ;
>   Navoient autre mancion."

ENGLAND.

Section XI.—Chaucer (1340-1400).

Authorities.—Ten Brink, 'Chaucer-Studien.' 1870. Furnivall, 'Trial-Forewords,' Chaucer Soc. Publ., 1871. Chaucer's 'Boëce,' ed. Morris. E.E.T.S., 1868. MS. in C. U. L., Ii. 3. 21* (early xv.)

But the middle-age writer upon whom, more than upon any other, Boethius left his mark, and with whom the English reader will probably feel most sympathy, is Geoffrey Chaucer, " the first founder and embellisher of ornate eloquence " in our language,

as Caxton reverently calls him.   His acquaintance
with the works of the Roman philosopher, which
would seem to date from about the year 1369, when
he wrote the 'Deth of Blaunche,' had ripened into a
real intimacy by the middle of the seventies and the
beginning of the eighties,—the period, that is, which
saw the production of 'Troylus and Cryseyde,' the
'Parlement of Foules,' the 'Hous of Fame,' and the
rendering into prose of the 'Consolation of Philosophy.'   At this time, indeed, Chaucer must have
known his Boethius almost by heart.   'Troylus and
Cryseyde' teems with echoes and direct imitations of
the Latin book, and Boethius is the *deus ex machinâ*
brought in by the poet to help him out of the difficulty into which his treatment of the story, so different from that of Boccaccio, had led him.   For
it will be remembered that the Italian poet in the
'Filostrato' hastens over the courtship of Troylus to
dwell upon the catastrophe and its after results,
while it is just upon the scenes which Boccaccio
neglected that Chaucer expended all his powers of
humour and pathos.   From Boccaccio we only get
one more illustration of the line, "Frailty, thy name
is woman"; from Chaucer a true love-story, the
most beautiful of the middle ages, and perhaps of
all time.

After Cryseyde has been wooed and won—in other words, when the poem has reached its culminating point of interest—Chaucer seems to shrink from the unwelcome task, which the development of the theme as he had it from Boccaccio set before him, of dragging his heroine in the dust; and so he calls in the aid of the 'Consolation' to account for her faithlessness.

> "For al that cometh, comth by necessite;
>   Thus to ben lorne, it is my desteyne,"

cries Troylus, when he learns that his love is to be parted from him and carried back to the Grecian camp; and he goes on in the words of Boethius (Cons., v. pr. 2 and 3) to show how God's fore-knowledge must of necessity destroy man's freewill, and that therefore Cryseyde and he, luckless pair, must accept and bow to the inevitable. He is interrupted in the midst of his meditations by Pandarus, and so never reaches the answer given by Philosophy to her imprisoned disciple, in which she tells him that the arm of God is not to be measured by the finger of man—that the divine prescience does not at all interfere with human freedom of choice. "Manet intemerata mortalibus arbitrii libertas" are among the last words she speaks to him. But to have developed the argument any further would have spoilt Chaucer's point : he wishes to excite compassion for his hero and heroine as the playthings of fortune and the victims of necessity.   And while we may question the artistic value of the explanation, we cannot deny that it serves its purpose well enough.   Cryseyde, with all her faults and weaknesses, is put beyond the reach of human criticism and reproof.

The translation of the ' De Consolatione ' comes no doubt, in point of time, before the great poem which has been engaging our attention ; but I am not at all disposed to subscribe to Mr Henry Morley's opinion that it is quite an early work. My reasons for venturing to differ from so high an authority will be best seen after a careful examination of the book : I shall accordingly reserve them till later.   It possesses a double interest for us,— first, as an example of fourteenth-century prose, and secondly, as an instance—the only known one—of Chaucer's method of literal translation.   I say advisedly literal translation, for although Chaucer often fails to catch the spirit of the Latin, he keeps, as a rule, so closely to the letter as to render necessary the interpolation of a multitude of glosses to make the meaning of many passages at all intelligible.   Indeed it is open to question whether the translator quite understood some of them himself. It would be very difficult, nay almost impossible, to say which of the explanations scattered broadcast over the pages of his ' Boece ' were inserted by him as he worked, and which he simply turned into English as he found them in the text. Three at least must have been present in the MS. used by Notker for his version.

	CHAUCER.	NOTKER.
i. m. 1	þe sorouful houre þat is to seyne þe deeþ.	Tíu léida stunda íh méino diu iúngesta.
i. pr. 1	A gregkysche **P** þat signifieþ _þe lijf actif. . . . **T** þat signi-fieþ þe lijf contemplatif.	Táz chríecheska p. táz pe-zéichenet practicam vitam táz chît activam. . . . Theta tíu bezéichenet theoreticam vitam daz chît contempla-tivam.
i. pr. 4	Þilk comaundement of picta-goras þat is to seyne men schal seruen to god and not to goddes.	Táz phitagoras phylosophus spráh de non sacris, aldé de non diis.[1]

These explanations seem to fall naturally into two great classes—

(*a*) Parenthetical—*i.e.*, those which in a modern book might stand in the text, but between brackets.

(*b*) Exegetical—*i.e.*, those which we should relegate to the notes.

As examples of the first of these classes, let us take the following :—

---

[1] The reading ἕπου θεῷ, ἀλλ' οὐ θεοῖς seems to have been an exceedingly common one in a certain family of MSS.

ii. pr. 1 (Morris, p. 32)[1]—

þe floor of fortune, þat is to seyn . . . worlde (*area fortunæ*).

iii. pr. 5 (M., p. 76)—

þe grete wey3t, þat is to sein of lordes power or fortune (*moles*).

iii. m. 8 (M., p. 81)—

þe shynynge of þi forme, þat is to seien þe beaute of þi body (*formæ nitor*).

iv. m. 1 (M., p. 111)—

þe swifte carte, þat is to seyne þe circuler moeuyng of the sonne (*volucrem currum*).

iv. m. 2 (M., p. 118)—

Wiþ so many wicked lordes, þat is to seyn wiþ so manye vices (*tot tyrannos*).

v. m. 1 (M., p. 152)—

By þilke lawe, þat is to sein by þe deuyne ordinaunce (*ipsa lege*).

v. pr. 6 (M., p. 175)—

It ne may nat unbytide as who seiþ it mot bitide (*non euenire non posse*).

The second class is a much smaller one, and therefore more easy to illustrate.

i. pr. 4 (M., p. 15)—

Theodoric's oppression.

Whan þat theodoric þe kyng of gothes in a dere 3er hadde hys gerners ful of corne and comaundede þat no man ne scholde bie no corne til his corne were solde and þat at a dere greuous pris.

i. pr. 4 (M., p. 15)—

Coemption.

Coempcioun þat is to seyn comune achat or bying to-gidere þat were establissed upon poeple by swiche a manere imposicioun as who so bou3te a busshel corn he moste geue the kyng þe fifte part.

---

[1] I quote from Dr Morris's edition of Boëce, E.E.T.S., 1868.

i. pr. 4 (M., p. 21)—

The popular opinion that prosperity implies goodness and misfortune wickedness. As þus þat yif a wyȝt haue prosperite he is a good man and worþi to haue þat prosperite. And who so haþ aduersite he is a wikked man, and god haþ forsake hym and he is worþi to haue þat aduersite.

ii. m. 1 (M., p. 33)—

Fortune likened to Euripus. Eurippe is an arm of þe see þat ebbith and flowiþ, and somtyme þe strem is on one syde and somtyme on þat oþer.

ii. pr. 2 (M., p. 35)—

A definition of tragedy. Tragedie is to seyne a dite of a prosperite for a tyme þat endiþ in wrechednesse.

ii. m. 7 (M., p. 60)—

Mors prima and mors secunda. þe first deeþ he clepiþ here þe departynge of þe body and þe soule. And þe secunde deeþ he clepeþ as here þe styntynge of þe renoun of fame.

iii. m. 10 (M., p. 94)—

God a refuge from the world. þis is to seyn, þat ȝe þat ben combred and deceyued wiþ worldely affecciouns comeþ now to þis souereyne good þat is god þat is refut to hem that wolen comyn to hym.

Now and again Chaucer recasts a whole passage, either because he was dissatisfied with his first attempt, or because he felt that the full force of the Latin could not be conveyed by a single rendering.

iii. pr. 1 (M., p. 63)—

So þat I trowe nat now þat I be unparygal to the strokes of fortune as who seyth I dar wel now suffren al the assautes of fortune.

Adeo ut iam me posthac inparem fortunæ ictibus esse non arbitrer.

iv. pr. 4 (M., p. 125)—

For þis þing þat I shal telle þe nowe ne shal not

seme lesse wondirful. But of þe þings þat ben
taken al so it is necessarie as ho seiþ it folweþ of
þat whiche þat is purposed byforn.

. . . *sed ex his quæ sumpta sunt æque est
necessarium.*

Besides these longer glosses there are innumerable alternative versions of single words belonging
by right to our class *A—maleficio* = malyfice or en-
chauntementz (M., p. 20); *imputare* = blamen ne
aretten (M., p. 40); *fœdera* = byndyng or alliaunce
(M., p. 159), &c., some of which possess a special
interest in that they discover the writer in the very
act of trying new words. Most have happily lived
on, and are in common use with us to-day; but
whether successful in his endeavour to enrich his
English vocabulary or not, Chaucer always displays
an excellent taste in his choice, and fully deserves
Caxton's word of praise which I quoted at the beginning of the section.

It is a thousand pities that " compotent," the opposite of impotent, did not take root in our language ;
and the modern writer on freewill would be grateful
for such a synonym as " arbitre " (*arbitrii libertas*).
In connection with this word and another, " au-
tumpne," which also appears here for the first time
in English, there is a point well worth remarking.
Each of them comes several times in the course

of the translation, and on the first occasion is left without comment. But when they occur again, Chaucer seems conscious that he is using words which after all require some explanation, and so he adds to the one, "that is to seyn the later ende of somer"; and to the other, "that is to seyn fre wille."

And now I have to perform the unpleasant duty of dressing a formal charge against Chaucer's scholarship. There will be two main counts in the indictment—

(1.) Actual misrendering of words.

(2.) Errors arising from constructions misunderstood.

Instances of (1) are—

i. pr. 4 (M., p. 16)—*Astrui*=lykned. This is perhaps a venial offence. I believe the right translation to be "added"; but it might possibly mean "opposed."

ii. pr. 5 (M., p. 48)—*Sepositis*=subgit.

iii. pr. 2 (M., p. 66)—*Afferre*=by-refte away.

iii. pr. 8 (M., p. 80)—*Obnoxius*=anoyously.

iii. pr. 8 (M., p. 81)—*Lyncei*=lynx (the beast, instead of Aristotle's Lynceus, the man).

iii. pr. 12 (M., p. 103)—*Clavus*=keye.

v. pr. 1 (M., p. 150)—*Principio*=prince.

v. pr. 1 (M., p. 151)—*Compendium*=abreggynge. The word here requires to be rendered "gain," although, of course, it sometimes means "abridgment."

The mistaken constructions are many and various.

Chaucer thrice translates active participles having reference to persons as if they were substantives :—

iii. pr. 4 (M., p. 74)—*Utentium* = usaunces.

iii. pr. 12 (M., p. 104)—*Detrectantium iugum* = a ȝok of mys-drawynges.

iii. pr. 12 (M., p. 104)—*Obtemperantium salus* = the sauynge of obedient þinges.

On the other hand, he sometimes gives to gerunds and substantives the force of participles referring to persons :—

ii. pr. 5 (M., p. 45)—*Effundendo* = to hem þat dispenden.

ii. pr. 5 (M., p. 45)—*Coacervando* = to hem þat mokeren.

iv. pr. 1 (M., p. 109)—*Facinorum* = wicked felouns.

The relation of the dependent to the principle sentence is a constant cause of stumbling :—

iii. pr. 9 (M., p. 83)—*Considera vero, re quod nihilo indigere, quod potentissimum, quod honore dignissimum esse concessum est; egere claritudinem quam sibi præstare non possit atque ob id aliqua ex parte uideatur abiectius.*

Considere þan quod she as we han grauntid her byforne þat he þat ne haþ nede of noþing and is most myȝty and most digne of honour yif hym nedeþ any clernesse of renoun which clernesse he myȝt nat graunten of hym self so þat for lakke of þilke clernesse he myȝt seme febler on any syde or þe more outcaste.

Here Chaucer has actually forgotten the main verb. A much needed gloss is appended to the passage, which saves the sense, but throws no light on the Latin construction.

iii. pr. 9 (M., p. 83)—*An tu arbitraris quod nihilo indigeat egere potentia?* Wenest þou þat he þat haþ nede of power þat hym ne lakkeþ no þing. (It is easy to see that *indigeat* and *egere* have changed places.)

On one occasion a word that should stand in the principal sentence is worked into the dependent:—

iii. pr. 7 (M., p. 79)—*Sed nimis e natura dictum est nescio quem filios invenisse tortores.* But it haþ ben seid þat it is ouer myche aʒeins kynde, &c.

As instances of promiscuous mistakes in translation I will take the following:—

ii. pr. 8 (M., p. 62)—*Fluctus auidum mare*=þe se so greedy to flowen.

iv. pr. 6 (M., p. 140)—*Quidam me quoque excellentior*=the moore excellent by me.

v. pr. 1 (M., p. 149)—*Auctoritate dignissima* = ful digne by authorite.

v. m. 3 (M., p. 159)—$\left\{\begin{array}{l}\textit{Sed cur tanto flagrat amore}\\ \textit{Veri tectas repperire notas}\end{array}\right\}$ =note of soþe y-couered.

v. pr. 4 (M., p. 162)—*Positionis gratia*=by grace of possessioun.

v. pr. 4 (M., p. 163)—*Quasi vero credamus*=ryʒt as we trowen.

v. m. 5 (M., p. 171)—*Male dissipis*=waxest yuel out of þi wit.

Over and above these grosser blunders, the translation bristles with what appear, to us at least, inappropriate or infelicitous renderings. Such are (a selection taken at random):—

i. m. 1 (M., p. 4)—*Laceræ camenæ*=rendyng muses.

i. m. 1 (M., p. 4)—*Ingratas moras*=a long unagreable dwellynges.

i. pr. 4 (M., p. 16)—*Alieni æris necessitudo*=necessity of foreine moneye.

i. m. 5 (M., p. 22)—*Solitas iterum mutet habenas* = comeþ eft
  aȝeynes hir used cours.

i. pr. 6 (M., p. 27)—*Velut hiante valli robore* = so as þe strengþe
  of þe paleys schynyng is open.

ii. pr. 1 (M., p. 31)—*Utere moribus* = use hir maners.

ii. pr. 5 (M., p. 45)—*Largiendi usu* = by usage of large ȝeuyng
  of hym þat haþ ȝeuen it.

ii. pr. 7 (M., p. 57)—*Commercii insolentia* = defaute of unusage
  entercommunyng of merchaundise.

iii. pr. 4 (M., p. 73)—*Multiplici consulatu* = many manere dignites
  of consules.

iii. pr. 12 (M., p. 105)—*Probationibus* . . . *ex altero fidem trahente*
  = proeues drawen to hem self hir feiþ and hir accorde
  eueriche of hem of oþer.

iii. m. 12 (M., p. 106)—*Silvas currere mobiles* = þe wodes meueble
  to rennen.

v. m. 5 (M., p. 176)—*Liquido volatu* = moist fleeyng.

It is, of course, not fair to reckon against the
translator those passages where he has been led
astray by a wrong reading in his text; but this is
a convenient place for recording them :—

i. m. 4—ἕπου θεῷ = men shal seruen to god and not to goddes.
  (The Cambridge MS. has " deo et non diis sacrifican-
  dum "—*vide supra*, p. 218).

ii. pr. 5 — *Postremo pulchritudinis* = the laste beaute.   (The
  Cambridge MS. reads " postreme.")

ii. m. 5 — *Arva* = armurers.   (The Cambridge MS. reads
  " arma.")

iii. pr. 11—*Sede* = feete.

iv. m. 7—*Immani* = empty.

Where now does this—to the general reader perhaps a little painful—examination of Chaucer's 'Boece'

lead us ? Not, I think, to the conviction that it is
a work of the author's early youth, a mere student's
exercise. It is surely most reasonable to connect its
composition with those poems which contain the
greatest number of recollections and imitations of its
original; and Chaucer's first efforts are guiltless of
these, while the writings of his middle and later
periods are full of them. Again, while no one can
deny that the translation abounds with slipshod
renderings, with awkward phrases and downright
glaring mistakes of a kind to make a modern
examiner's hair stand on end, yet its inaccuracy and
infelicity is not that of an inexperienced Latin
scholar, but rather of one who was no Latin scholar
at all. Given a man who is sufficiently conversant
with a language to read it fluently without paying
too much heed to the precise value of participle and
preposition, who has the wit and the sagacity to
grasp the meaning of his author, but not the intimate
knowledge of his style and manner necessary to a
right appreciation of either, and—especially if he set
himself to write in an uncongenial and unfamiliar
form—he will assuredly produce just such a result
as Chaucer has done. We must now glance at the
literary style of the translation. As Ten Brink has
observed, we can here see as clearly as in any work

of the middle ages what a high cultivation is re-
quisite for the production of a good prose.[1] Verse,
and not prose, is the natural vehicle for the expression of every language in its infancy, and it is
certainly not in prose that Chaucer's genius shows
to best advantage. The restrictions of metre were
indeed to him as silken fetters, while the freedom of
prose only served to embarrass him; just as a bird
that has been born and bred in captivity, whose
traditions are all domestic, finds itself at a sad loss
when it escapes from its cage and has to fall back
on its own resources for sustenance. In reading
'Boece,' we have often as it were to pause and look
on while Chaucer has a desperate wrestle with a
tough sentence; but though now he may appear to
be down, with a victorious knee upon him, next
moment he is on his feet again, disclaiming defeat in
a gloss which makes us doubt whether his adversary
had so much the best of it after all. But such
strenuous endeavour, even when it is crowned with
success, is strange in a writer one of whose chief
charms is the delightful ease, the complete absence
of effort, with which he says his best things. It
is only necessary to compare the passages of Boethius
in the prose version with the same when they re-

[1] *Op. cit.*, p. 141.

appear in the poems, to realise how much better they look in their verse dress.

Let the reader take Troylus's soliloquy on Freewill and Predestination (book iv. st. 134-148) and read it side by side with the corresponding passage in 'Boece' (M., pp. 152-159), and he cannot fail to feel the superiority of the former to the latter. With what clearness and precision does the argument unfold itself, how close is the reasoning, how vigorous and yet graceful is the language!

It is to be regretted that Chaucer did not do for all the metra of the 'Consolation' what he did for the fifth of the second book. A solitary gem like "The Former Age" makes us long for a whole set.

Sometimes, whether unconsciously or of set purpose it is difficult to decide, his prose slips into verse :—

" It likeþ me to shew by subtil songe
  Wiþ slakke and delitable soun of strenges " (iii. m. 2).
" Whan fortune wiþ a proude ryȝt hand " (ii. m. 1).
      " And þat þe leest isle in þe see
        þat hyȝt tile be þral to þe " (iii. m. 5).

And there are instances where he actually reproduces the original Latin metre :—

" O ȝe my frendes what or wherto auaunted ȝe me to be weleful
  For he þat haþ fallen stood not in stedfast degree " (i. m. 1).
        " Weyne þou joie
          Drif fro þe drede
          Fleme þou hope " (i. m. 7).

" He ȝaf to þe sonne hys bemes
  He ȝaf to þe moone hir hornes
  He ȝaf þe men to the erþe
  He ȝaf the sterres to þe heuene
  He encloseþ wiþ membres þe soules
  þat comen fro hys heye sete.
  þanne comen all mortal folk of noble seed
        Whi noysen ȝe or bosten of ȝoure eldris " (iii. m. 6).

Section XII.—John the Chaplain
(early fifteenth century).

Authorities.—Warton's 'History of English Poetry' (1774-81),
vol. ii., sec. 2.   Todd's 'Illustrations of the Lives and Writings of
Gower and Chaucer' (1810).   MSS. in B. M., 18 a. xiii.* (early xv.);
Harl. 43 (xv$\frac{1}{2}$.); Harl. 44 (xv$\frac{1}{2}$); Sl. 554 (xv$\frac{1}{4}$).

The reader will remember that we settled the
probable date of Chaucer's 'Boëce' to be somewhere
about 1380.   Before another generation had passed,
the hand of the translator was busy once more with
the 'Consolation.'   This time it is a verse rendering
into eight-line stanzas, made in 1410 by a certain
Johannes Capellanus.   It is not easy to establish
this writer's identity.   For while the majority of
MSS. are simply signed with the above name and
designation, a copy of the book printed at Tavistock
in 1525 qualifies the author as Johannes Waltunen
(John Walton); one MS. further states that he was
canon of Osney;[1] and another calls him, not Walton,

[1] Hearne, Præf. in Camdeni Annales, p. 133.

but Tebaud *alias* Watyrbeche.[1] The balance of
evidence seems in favour of John Walton, who
undertook the translation at the request of Dame
Elisabeth Berkeley. It is at least certain that
Johannes Capellanus is not John Lydgate, as Peiper,
led astray perhaps by the B. M. Catalogue, affirms.
The translator, whoever he was, did his work well, so
far as I am able to judge from a cursory examination
of the manuscripts in London. The student of our
literary history will note with interest a passage in
the prologue where the writer acknowledges his debt
to Chaucer, and modestly disclaims all wish or power
to compete with him or Gower:—

> " I have herd spek, and sumwhat have yseyn
>   Of diverse men þat woundir subtyllye
>   In metir sum and sum in prose pleyn
>   This book translated have full suffishauntlye
>   Into englissh tonge word for word well nye
>   Bot I most use the wittes þat I have
>   Þogh y may noght do so, yit noght for thye
>   With help of God þe sentence shall I save.
>
>   To Chaucer þat is floure of rethoryk
>   In Englisshe tong and excellent poete
>   This wot I wel no þing may I do lyk
>   Þogh so þat I of makynge entyrmete[2]
>   And Gower þat so craftily doth trete
>   As in his book of moralite
>   Þogh I to þeym in makyng am unmete
>   Ʒit most I shewe it forth þat is in me."

---

[1] Todd's Illustrations of Gower and Chaucer, Introd., p. 31.
[2] Entremettre.

But the importance of the translation does not lie, as far as our present purpose is concerned, in its literary merit, so much as in the fact that when the only poet of the reign of Henry IV.[1] took up his song, the theme should once more be the ' Consolation of Philosophy.'

For the sake of consistency, let me give the first and last stanzas of ii. m. 5 as a specimen of John the Chaplain :—

> " Full wonder blisseful was þat raþer age
> When mortal men couthe holde hymself payed
> To fede þeym self wit oute suche outerage
> Wiþ mete þat trewe feldes have arrayed
> Wiþ acorne þaire hunger was alayed
> And so þei couthe sese þaire talent
> Thei had yit no queynt craft assayed
> As clarry for to make ne pyment.
>
> .   .   .   .
>
> I wold our tyme might turne certanly
> And þise maneres alwey wit us dwelle
> But loue of hauyng brenneþ fervently
> More fersere þan þe veray fuyre of helle
> Allas who was þat man þat wold him melle
> This gold and gemmes that were keuered
> Þat first began to myne y can not telle
> Bot þat he fond a parelous precious."

---

[1] *Vide* Warton, *op. cit.*, p. 34.

ITALY.

Section XIII.—Alberto della Piagentina (fl. 1332)
and others.

Authorities.—Argelati, ' Biblioteca degli Volgazarizzatori.' Milan, 1767. Tiraboschi, 'Storia della Letteratura Italiana,' t. iv. and v. Florence, 1806-7.

The merits of Boethius received a more tardy recognition in the land of his birth, and apparently it was not until the fourteenth century was fairly on its course that an Italian translator took the field. It is true that Brunetto Latino, the great Florentine encyclopædist, the teacher of Dante, was accredited by Voigt,[1] on whose authority I know not, with a vernacular translation of 'Boethius.' I should not take the trouble to notice this error, which was exploded more than a hundred years ago, if Peiper had not perpetuated it in his list of *interpretes.*[2] The assertion that Brunetto translated the ' De Consolatione ' was made in the first volume of Argelati's ' Biblioteca,' only to be retracted in the fifth.[3] And if his evidence and that of Tiraboschi[4] is not

[1] Wiederbeleburg des Klassischen Alterthums, p. 13 : Berlin, 1880.

[2] *Op. cit.*, p. 54.   [3] i. p. 170 ; v. p. 429.
[4] *Op. cit.*, t. iv. 477.

considered sufficiently convincing, let Thor Sundby's
silence be added thereto, and there is little doubt
upon which side the balance will kick the beam.
The Danish professor, who is the final authority for
Brunetto Latino, does not say a word about any
such translation.[1]   The mistake seems to have arisen
from the fact that in a book published by Manni
of Florence in 1735 Brunetto's 'Motti de' Filosofi'
is found in close connection with a 'Boezio della
Consolazione   Volgarizzato   da   Maestro   Alberto
Fiorento.'   We may confidently identify this translator with the Alberto della Piagentina who thus
beguiled the hours of his incarceration at Venice in
1332.

> " Io sono Alberto della Piagentina
> Di che Firenze vera Donna fue
> Che nel mille trecento trentadue
> Volgarizzai questa eccelsa Dottrina
> E per larghezza di grazia divina
> Ne chiosai due libri et piue
> Anzi che morte coll' opere sue
> In carcere mi desse disciplina,"

he writes; and although he does not further en-
lighten us as to who he was, or why he was put in
prison, still it is pleasant to think that Boethius's

---

[1] B. L.'s Levnet og Skrifter, Copenhagen, 1869, of which there
is an Italian translation by Renier : Florence, 1884.

words could afford comfort and relief to this later tenant of an Italian dungeon.[1]

Argelati's list contains as many as ten trans-lations [2] in manuscript, presumably before the fifteenth century, of whose different authors we know absolutely nothing, save that one was Fra Giovanni da Foligno, and another Messer Grazia da Siena, who undertook this work at the request of Nicolò di Guio in 1343.

Three other translators of the 'De Consolatione' before the Renaissance—a Greek, a Spaniard, and a German—claim a passing notice.

The first of these, both in point of time and interest, is Maximus Planudes.

GREECE.

SECTION XIV.—MAXIMUS PLANUDES (fl. 134–).

Authorities. — Fabricius, 'Bibl. Græca' (ed. Harles), tom. xi. C. F. Weber, 'Carmina A. M. T. S. Boetii Græce conversa per

---

[1] Tiraboschi (*op. cit.*, t. v. p. 623) is inclined to identify him with Albertino da Piacenza, professor of grammar at Bologna in 1315.

[2] Among them is mentioned "four books of the Consolation, translated by Brunetto Latino." The value of the entry will be best appreciated by Argelati's own note : "Stà nella Bibl. Maglia-becchiana, come dall' Indice de MSS. che abbiamo riportato della medesima, e dalle nostre vecchie Schede, nelle quali notammo d'averlo veduto, e nulla di più."

Maximum Planudem.' Darmstadt, 1833. C. F. Weber, 'Dissertatio de latine scriptis,' &c.   Cassel, 1852.   E. A. Bétant, 'De la Cons. de la Phil.,' Traduction grecque de Maxime Planude.   Geneva, 1871.

The rendering into his native Greek of the ' Consolation ' is no discredit to the reputation of the learned monk of Constantinople, the compiler of the ' Anthology.'   In it he shows himself a very skilful versifier, turning the various numbers of Boethius into their appropriate metres.   There is a satisfaction in finding that right in the middle of the fourteenth century—we have reason to believe that Planudes lived till at least 1352—Greek verses were being written, which, if they are deficient in the finer qualities of the old poetry, are still dexterous and graceful.

The following lines, the beginning and end of ii. m. 5, are copied from Weber's edition :—

> Ὡς ὄλβιος ὢν ὁ πρὶν αἰών,
> μικροῖς ἀγαπῶν πεδίοσι
> σπατάλαις τ' οὐκ ἔκλυτος ἄρχαις
> σχεδίην τ' εἰς βουλυτὸν ἠθὰς
> 5 δαιτ' ἀκροδρύοισι ποιεῖσθαι.
>
> .   .   .   .   .
>
> 25 αὖτ' ὀξύτερος πυρὸς Αἴτνης
> φιλοχρηματίης πόθος αὔξει
> φεῦ, τις πέλε πρῶτος, ὅς ἄχθος
> χρυσοῖο καλυπτομένοιο
> κρύπτειν τε λίθους ἐθελόντας
> σεπτὸν μάλα πῆμ' ἀνόρυξεν ;

SPAIN.

Section XV.—Fra Antonio Ginebreda.

Authorities.—-Amat, 'Diccionario de los escritores Catalanes.' Barcelona, 1836. Incunable in Mus. Brit., 'Boecio, De Consolacion.' Sevilla, 1511.

Peiper's words (*op. cit.*, p. lv) would lead one to suppose that there was no other Spanish translator of our author before 1500. But the prologue to the Seville edition of 1511 describes how the present version was undertaken at the request of a young noble of Valencia, " porque obra tan solenne no remaniesse imperfecta "; and mentions, among other foregoing translations, one, which left much to be desired, dedicated to the Infante of Mallorca.[1]

There is little to record of this Fra Antonio beyond the fact that he was a Dominican, and an ornament to his order, who died in 1395, but not before he had turned all the works of Boethius into Catalan. So at least says Amat (*op. cit.*, p. 295), although I have not been able to find cause why Fra Antonio should be credited with more than the rendering of the ' Consolation.'

[1] I take it this prologue was prefixed to the first edition, 1493. It can hardly be that Fra Antonio is covertly attacking his own work.

That this rendering, despite its writer's preten-
sions, is far from perfect, will readily be seen from
the following excerpt (ii. m. 5) :—

"Tan buena era la vida de los premeros habi-
tadores del mundo : que solamente querian aquellas
cosas que eran necessarias a la vida e no querian
superfluydad de vestes [1] ni de viandas : ni de re-
quezas," &c.

GERMANY.

SECTION XVI.—PETER OF KASTL.

Authorities. — Pezius, 'Thesaurus Anecdotorum Novissimus'
('Dissertatio Isagogica' in tomum iv. p. xxiv),[2] 1723. Andreas,
'Chronicon Generale' (in Pezius, *lib. cit.*)

In the year 1401 Peter, Presbyter in Kastl, a
Benedictine monk, is said to have written a translation of the 'De Consolatione.' Pezius, I know not
on what grounds, suspects this to be the one which
was printed, together with the Latin text and St

[1] A worm has made its hole through the middle of this word in
the B. M. copy. I have restored it to the best of my ability.

[2] With the memory of a fatiguing *chasse au renvoi* fresh on me, I
cannot resist entering a protest against Peiper's method of referring
to Pezius. All the information he vouchsafes the unfortunate
reader at this point is "Pezius's Anecd., p. xxiiii." Now, as the
Anecdotorum Thesaurus is a vast work in six ponderous folios, to
each one of which is prefixed an introductory dissertation, paged in

Thomas Aquinas's Commentary, by Coburger at
Nuremberg in 1473. Peter seems to have been
more successful as a literal translator than the
Spaniard we have been discussing :—

"O wie gar vil selig ist gewesen das vorder alter
das sich liess benügen an den getrewen veldern, und
nicht ward verderbet mit der tregen oder unertigen
überflüssigkeit, ungewont helte zeprechen das spat
vasten mit der leichten aicheln . . . 25 Aber die
inprünstig lieb zehaben das gut ist frayssamer dann
das fewr des perges Ethna. Ach wer ist der erst
gewesen unter den die gewollet haben das die
gewicht des verborgen goldes und die edeln gesteyn
solten verporgen beleiben. Wann der hat begraben
hohgultig oder achtbar scheden."

I have little doubt that other Germans besides
Notker and Peter of Kastl tried their hand on
Boethius, but I have not been able so far to find a
trace of them.

Roman numerals, it involved no little time, and the turning of many
leaves, to realise that p. xxiiii meant the twenty-fourth page of the
Dissertatio Isagogica in tomum quartum. While I am on this subject, I may perhaps be allowed to call attention to the same editor's
description of the MS. of the Consolation and Tracts in the Rehdiger Library at Breslau. He calls it simply " Rehdigerianus " (op.
cit., p. xiiii). Without doubt Thomas von Rehdiger (ob. 1576) was
a great man, but strangers can hardly be expected to know instinc-
tively that he founded a library (the Elisabeth-Bibliothek) in the
town from which he took his name !

The beginning of the fifteenth century is in more than one way a convenient limit to set to this list of vernacular translations. But it must not be supposed that the story of Boethius's influence on medieval literature is nearly told yet. I protest I am appalled at the amount I have left unsaid. He had a host of imitators in Latin, some of whom, such as Bernard Silvester, Alain de Lille, John de Gerson, Alphonso de la Torre, cannot be passed over in silence without regret. Much might be written about Boethius and Dante, and perhaps an explanation offered of the statement in the 'Convito' that the Roman philosopher was not known to many; [1] while to collect the references to Boethius in the 'Roman de la Rose,' the great 'Ars Amoris' of the middle ages, would necessitate an appendix longer than that which I have devoted to Chaucer. The same, though in a less degree, would, I fancy, hold good of Gower. Lastly, it remains to be seen how far such combinations of verse and prose as the 'Vita Nuova,' the 'Ameto' of Boccaccio, or the 'Voir dit' of Guillaume de Machault, were inspired by the 'Consolation of Philosophy.' The subject is indeed fresher and altogether more attractive than that of the present chapter; but then it requires a

[1] See Morris in Chaucer's Boëce, p. ii, note.

far wider knowledge of medieval literature than I can lay claim to. And I feel that I have already used enough paper and tried my reader's patience too far. One word, however, must be said, before taking leave of Boethius, touching his connection with scholasticism.

CHAPTER VII.

BOETHIUS AND THE SCHOLASTIC PROBLEM.

Authorities.—First and foremost, Hauréau s admirable 'Histoire de la Philosophie Scolastique' (Paris, 1850), tome i., to which I owe more than can be recorded here. I have also consulted Cousin, 'Histoire de la Philosophie au xviiie siècle,' 9me leçon ; Prantl, 'Geschichte der Logik' (Leipzic, 1855-70) ; Maurice's 'Medieval Philosophy' (London, 1857) ; and the first Appendix to Grote's 'Aristotle on the Theory of Universals.'

I HAVE already hinted at the paramount influence exercised by Boethius in his writings other than the 'Consolation' on the philosophy of the middle ages known to us under the name of the scholastic philosophy. If we would have a clear conception of this much-abused and much-misunderstood term, we must go back to its literal meaning, being before all things careful to have our minds free from the

weight of prejudice that has gathered against it
during the last four hundred years—a prejudice
which rose with the intellectual revolt of the Renaissance, and culminated in the flippancy and in-
tolerance of the eighteenth century. Scholastic,
then, means simply *taught in the schools*—in those
schools which received their charter of foundation
in the celebrated letter of Charlemagne, written in
787 to the bishops of France, wherein he recommends an immediate return to the long-neglected
study of secular learning. In the numerous ecclesiastical seminaries that sprang up in answer to this
call—at Tours, at Lyons, at Orléans, at St Gall,
Reichenau, Ferrières, and elsewhere—the course of
instruction was confined at the outset to writing,
singing, and grammar.

Grammar soon brought in its train the sister arts
of poetry and rhetoric. But if these last were
looked upon with suspicion by the Church as dangerous, and conducive to the forbidden commerce
with paganism, it would take yet longer to win her
to a recognition of philosophy. Thus the seed sown
by Charlemagne lay for more than a hundred years
without any apparent promise of bringing forth.
In the secular school of the Palace it was different.
There the king had given Alcuin the Saxon and

Clement the Irishman full leave to share with their pupils, without fear of ecclesiastical interference, all the treasures of pagan learning to which they had the key; and so it is there that we first find in force that familiar distribution of the arts and sciences into the *trivium* and the *quadrivium*—the former comprising grammar, rhetoric, and dialectic, the latter arithmetic, geometry, music, and astronomy— which made the beaten track for so many generations of teachers. We are here only concerned with the third branch of the *trivium*, dialectic—the foundation-stone on which the mighty edifice of medieval thought was reared. Before considering how that foundation-stone was laid, or what part our author had in its preparation, we must understand what the scholastic philosophy was, what were its aims and objects. It was not an elementary doctrine, as some [1] have supposed, to which the Schoolmen resorted as a solution of the difficulties that confronted them on the threshold of knowledge; for under its shadow every imaginable doctrine found its ardent partisans. It was not simply theology in another guise—theology militant, as distinguished from theology contemplative and mystic; for although its propounders were in all instances monks—to the

---

[1] *E.g.*, Tennemann in his Manual, vol. viii.

clergy alone was the responsibility of education
intrusted—and although from time to time one of
their number, from an excess of zeal for his calling,
might be led to overstep the bounds that separate
philosophy and theology, still the line of demarca-
tion was, as a rule, carefully enough respected. It
is true that when the upper air of metaphysics is
reached, the philosophy and the theology of the
Schoolmen do blend and merge themselves one in
the other; but that is just because contemplation of
the essence of being is the very summit of both
these sciences. The primary object of the scholastic
philosophy was an application of the doctrines of
Aristotle to all problems of thought. We must
remember that it was not by any means the real
Aristotle whom these early doctors knew and followed, whose authority they cited with an almost
religious awe, but an Aristotle moulded, and sometimes distorted, to suit the translator's mood, at first
in the works of Porphyry and Boethius, and afterwards in those of the Arabs, Averrhoës and Avicenna.
Till towards the end of the tenth century the Stagyrite was only known by a part of the 'Organon,' the
' De Interpretatione,' translated by Boethius, and the
same writer's edition of Porphyry's 'Introduction to
the Categories.'

The treatise on the 'Categories' falsely attributed to Augustine, which had for some time the credit of being a translation, was a mere abridgment.   By the end of the century, however, we find it replaced by the authentic translation of the Roman philosopher, but even then the book was a rare one. When the grammarian Gunzo in 957 displayed his library before the admiring eyes of the monks of St Gall, he did not number an example of the 'Categories' among his hundred volumes.   But that it did exist at this time is testified by Richer the chronicler, who states that about 985 Gerbert of Rheims was lecturing on the 'Introduction,' the 'Interpretation,' and the 'Categories' from the text of Boethius.   These, together with the 'Timæus' of Plato, formed the whole of the old Greek philosophical library of the schools until the middle of the twelfth century, when it was enriched by the addition of all the works of Aristotle, translated from the Arabic into Latin, and brought from Spain by certain learned Jews.   But though the true Aristotle was absent all this time, it must not be supposed that therefore the teaching of logic according to his methods was impossible.   The want was supplied by some original tracts of Boethius—the " De Divisione," the " De Syllogismo Hypothetico," the " De Definitione," and the like—which contained *en abrégé* most of the doctrines of the Stagyrite.

I have said that the principle of the scholastic philosophy was an application of Aristotelianism to problems of thought. The particular question which we are accustomed to associate with the middle ages is the one of the nature of genera and species. It must not be imagined that this great problem, which was to exercise the minds of the Schoolmen for nearly six centuries, rose and died with their system. It is one which, in the admirable words of Cousin, " à toutes les époques, tourmente et féconde l'esprit humain, et, par les diverses solutions qu'il soulève, engendre toutes les écoles." [1] It underlies the vague and unsystematic speculations of the early Eleatics, it begins to take form in the doctrines of Parmenides and Heraclitus, but it first finds its proper place in the colloquies of Socrates and the teaching of Plato. While Socrates subjected it to close analytical inquiry, it was left to his disciple Plato to maintain the real existence of universals apart from any subjective cognition—in a word, to assert the doctrine of Realism in its fullest and most unqualified extension. He taught that there existed in the world above us an idea, an archetype of every

[1] Introd. aux œuvres inédites d'Abélard, p. 68.

thing in the visible world; that these ideas alone were stable and permanent—that, indeed, they were the only true and knowable realities; that particulars were but shadowy copies of these eternal forms, and were knowable only by reason of their resemblance to them.

This is the theory which the Schoolmen succinctly described in the phrase, " Universalia extra et ante rem." Its great danger lay in the wide gulf it placed between the world of thought and the world of sense, in its complete separation of the universal from the particular. Aristotle set himself in strong opposition to his master on this point, and approached the question from quite a different direction. Instead of working downwards from that which is most general to that which is most particular, he works upwards from the particular to the general, and places reality in the individual alone— the universal being a mere predicate of the particular. And predicates have no separate reality of their own, but only an adjective reality as accompaniments and determinants.[1]

The question, as brought before the notice of the early Schoolmen in Porphyry's [2] ' Introduction to the

[1] Grote's Aristotle, App. I., p. 264. Aristotle, Metaphysics.
[2] 270-300 A.D.

Categories of Aristotle,' ranged itself under three
heads : (1) Do genera and species subsist, possess a
real existence ? or do they consist in the simple
conception of the subject ?   (2) If subsistent, are
they corporeal or incorporeal ?   (3) If corporeal,
are they separate from sensible objects ? or do they
reside in these objects, forming something coexistent
with them ?   Porphyry, indeed, has no sooner pro-
pounded these questions to his friend and pupil
Chrysaorius, than he sets them aside as being altogether too profound for present investigation—
" altissimum enim negotium est huiusmodi et
maioris egens inquisitionis."   In other words, he
refers them to metaphysics—to a branch of philosophy higher than that upon which he is for the
moment engaged.   But the students of the eighth
and ninth centuries, who were first introduced to
his work by Boethius, had no very clear conception
of the exact province of metaphysics ; and, knowing
intuitively that this question of the nature of
universals lay at the root of all inquiry, they
could not waive it with the same unconcern.   From
Boethius, indeed, they might not expect any clearer
utterance on the subject.   Like Porphyry, he
refrains from giving vent to the expression of a
definite opinion.   Two commentaries from his pen

on the Greek philosopher's 'Isagoge' have come
down to us, the first based upon the translation by
Victorinus, the second upon a new translation of his
own.   There is so much in this second and longer
effort that is in seeming contradiction to the first,
that the reader may well be momentarily at a loss
to determine with which side Boethius casts his lot,
—whether with the Realist or with the Nominalist.
The event will show us that it is with neither the
one nor the other.   If he had rested content with his
first commentary, we should have been compelled to
rank him with the former.   For, commenting on
the evasive answer given by Porphyry to the question of the nature of genera and species, he distinctly says, " If you weigh the truth and correctness
of things, it is impossible to doubt that genera and
species really are."

  That is to all appearance as candid a confession
of Realism as Plato himself could have desired.
And it has led so careful and profound a thinker
as Maurice [1] to the conviction that Boethius decided
in favour of Realism.

  Souvent homme varie, however, and if a change
of opinion were at any time permissible, it would
surely be when one is dealing with the subtle and

[1] *Op. cit.*, p. 11.

dangerous problems suggested by species and genera. The very fact that Boethius was at the trouble of translating Porphyry anew on his own account, and of writing a second commentary on the same, proves that he was dissatisfied with his first essay. We should indeed be justified in disregarding altogether the two immature and incomplete dialogues on Porphyry, and giving our undivided attention to the five books of commentary. But in reality there is no need for this, since, as has been pointed out by both Rémusat and Hauréau, all that Boethius wishes to establish on the one and the other occasion is the fact that every predicate subsists within and conjoined to the thing of which it is predicated, and not without or separated from it; that things are substances, and that every substance is individual.

When he attacks the problem for the second time, he casts aside all doubtful formulas, and states in the clearest language that, according to Aristotle, genus is not a thing, because a thing is necessarily one in number, whereas it (genus) is common to more than one. But, object the Realists, who derive the particular from the universal, numerical unity is not the necessary condition of essence, and genera and species are essences which embrace a variety

of similar beings. To this objection Boethius replies
in the words of Aristotle : If genera exist in virtue
of their essential existence, this existence cannot be
denied to that which contains them—namely, the
genus generalissimum ; hence genera are not in
themselves beings, *entia,* but parts of the whole
which embraces them. Now that which is one
by nature is not divisible into parts, and so this
whole which alone exists does not contain the
genera : these, therefore, can have no existence.

As genera and species were the prime causes of
the great middle-age controversy, the theme on which
so many and different variations were woven, it is
expedient to hear more particularly what our author
has to say about them. The passage containing the
ultimate expression of his teaching on this subject is
to be found towards the end of the first book of the
commentary on his own translation of ' Porphyry.'
It is all too long to quote in its entirety ; on the
other hand, it would be dangerous to attempt a summary of such close and compact reasoning. I must
therefore crave the reader's indulgence while I endeavour, by a judicious mingling of direct translation
and compressed paraphrase, to set before him the
opinion of Boethius on the scholastic problem.

" Since every conception arises from some object

to which it conforms, the conception of genera and species arises from an object, and must conform to it. They therefore do not merely reside in the intelligence, they exist in the reality of things. A conception which differs from reality is false; therefore, if the conception of genera and species arising out of reality does not conform to this reality, it must be false. We do not say that every conception is false which is not identical with the object from which it comes. It is only the conception of the union of two things that are by nature separate, such as a man and a horse united to form a centaur, that is false. By the process of abstraction and division we can realise a conception which does not conform to reality and yet is not false. Here it is no longer to the senses but to the mind that we must trust. For example, the mind can separate from the body and endow with existence such a thing as a line, which has no sensible existence apart from the body. In this way it is enabled to contemplate the incorporeal which is contained within, and owes its existence to, the corporeal. Now genera and species are contained or within corporeals or within incorporeals. If they are presented to the mind as contained within incorporeals, an incorporeal idea is at once formed. If they are presented to the mind as adherent to corporeals, they

can be abstracted and contemplated by themselves.
It cannot be said that we have a false idea of a line
because we contemplate it apart from the body to
which it owes its existence.   Genus, species, line,
then, exist in corporeal and sensible things, but to
understand their real nature we must conceive them
apart from sensibles.   Moreover, they are contained
in particular objects, although they are known as
universals.   Species is only a conception formed
from the substantial resemblance of a number of dis-
similar individuals; genus is only a conception
formed from the resemblance of a number of dis-
similar species.   This resemblance is *sensible* when
it appears in the particular, it is *intelligible* when it
appears in the universal.   Universality and par-
ticularity have one and the same object; but it is
universal when it is intelligibly conceived, it is particular when it is sensibly perceived in the things to
which it owes its existence.   Genera and species are
in one way things and in another way conceptions,
and in this sense they are incorporeal; and they are
then conceived apart from bodies, as subsisting by
themselves and not by anything else.   According to
Plato, genera and species are not merely conceptions
in so far as they are universals; they are real things
existing apart from bodies.   According to Aristotle,

they are conceived as incorporeals in so far as they are universals, but they have no real existence apart from the sensible world."

It is to Aristotle's opinion that Boethius inclines, although, as I have said, he refuses to commit himself any further than Porphyry. He tells us himself that he considers it unseemly (*non aptum*) to decide between Plato and Aristotle. His position is happily described by Godefroi de Saint-Victor[1] (twelfth century), who represents him as preserving a discreet silence over the lively dispute between the two great philosophers :—

> " Assidet Boethius, stupens de hac lite,
> Audiens quid hic et hic asserat perite,
> Et quid cui faveat non discernit rite,
> Nec præsumit solvere litem definite."

But an eclectic suspension of judgment of this kind was not likely to satisfy the Schoolmen, with their burning anxiety to know the why and wherefore of all knowledge ; nor would they be content to run in the safe middle way traced for them by all the commentators of Aristotle, from Porphyry to Boethius. And although in the eighth and ninth centuries Hrabanus Maurus and Eric of Auxerre steadfastly upheld the Aristotelian tradition, the standard of Realism was presently unfurled by Johannes

[1] Quoted by Hauréau, *op. cit.*, i. p. 120.

Scotus Erigena, who came in the course of the ninth
century to the court of Charles the Bald, filled
with a vast enthusiasm for Plato, and a sovereign
contempt for Boethius and all his school. In his
enthusiasm he carried the realistic teaching of his
master to the last extreme, and revived the old
doctrine of *universalia ante et extra rem*. I have no
time to devote to a study of this extraordinary man,
who flashed like a meteor out of the darkest hour of
the middle ages, and I must confine myself to a
statement of my conviction that he was an earnest
Christian, whose primary object was not to merge
God and His Creation in one, but to keep the two
apart,—to distinguish the divine from the human
nature. But in his fierce wrestle with the logical
formulas that chained and bound the Absolute and
the Eternal, he found himself dangerously near the
verge of Pantheism.

Hear his words on the nature of God : " When we
are told that God is the maker of all things, we are
simply to understand that God is in all things—that
He is the substantial essence of all things. He, and
He alone, really exists through and in Himself ; He,
and He alone, resumes in Himself all that resides in
those things to which existence is attributed. Nothing
of the things that are exists in reality through itself ;

but all things owe whatever in them is rightly understood to be to Him only who alone exists through Himself." In other words, he maintained that reality only resided in the incorporeal universal from which sensible individuals are derived. Whatever may be the errors into which the bold speculations of Erigena led him, we see that he did not shrink from a systematic and methodical review of all the questions which had received such opposite treatment at the hands of the followers of Plato and Aristotle respectively. One side or the other was eagerly espoused by the philosophers of his own and the succeeding ages, some of whom, like Remigius of Auxerre, followed the Irishman far enough, but shrank from his uncompromising profession of Realism. Others combated the teaching to the uttermost, without, however, bestowing a word of praise or blame on the teacher. The reason of this resolute silence on the part of friends and enemies alike is the fact that certain of his utterances on Grace and on the Eucharist savoured of heresy, and were condemned as dangerous to the faithful. It was not until the twelfth century that a voice, that of Wilbald of Cowey, was uplifted in defence of the greatest metaphysician of the middle ages.

We are now standing on the shore of the great

scholastic controversy.   It is not within our power,
if it were our desire, to set out on a voyage of
inquiry on that deep and dangerous ocean.   Let it
suffice that we have seen the question of the nature
of universals fairly launched by Porphyry and
Boethius his translator, who provided a Latin no-
menclature which, in the prevailing ignorance of
Greek, was absolutely indispensable.   But before we
turn away from the scholastic philosophy, a word
must be said upon its value in the history of thought.
Although it was fated, together with all the subjects
of that fierce debate, to fade and fall away, giving
place to the new inductive spirit of the sixteenth
century, it must not on that account be regarded as
a useless and withered system.   The middle ages,
the dark ages as we have been taught to call
them, were the period of silent preparation and
steady self-teaching which must necessarily inter-
vene between the death of an old world and the
birth of a new.   During such a period originality of
thought and expression is rare, if not impossible :
it is in the original treatment of a well-worn theme
that the greatest minds show forth, and there are few
greater in the history of philosophy than Johannes
Scotus, Thomas Aquinas, and Dante Alighieri.

APPENDIX A.

SYNOPSIS OF MSS. OF THE THEOLOGICAL TRACTS.

This table is based on the lists furnished by Peiper and Usener. I have added four manuscripts—one in the British Museum and another in the Cambridge University Library, and two in the Public Library at Orléans.

A.—MS. containing tr. i., ii., iii., iv., and v., in which iv. appears with the regular title A. M. T. S. B. ex cons. ord. patric., &c.

Einsiedeln, 235 (cent. x. or xi.)
   Here, contrary to the usual order, iv. follows immediately on i.

B.—MSS. containing only tr. i., ii., iii., and iv., in which iv. appears without title.

1. Tegeernsee, 765 (now at Munich, Lat. 18,765), (x.)
   According to Usener (*op. cit.*, p. 56), this MS. has lost v. by mere accident.
2. Paris, Bibl. Reg. MSS. Lat. 1919 (xiv.), (Cat. cod. MSS. &c., Paris, 1744). ? title *eiusdem.*

C.—MSS. containing tr. i., ii., iii., iv., and v., in which iv. appears without title.

1. Bern., 510 (ix.-x.)
2. Mus. Brit. Harl., 3095 (x.)
3. Florent. s. Croce, 23, 12 (x.)

4. Florent. Ambros. (x.)
5. Orléans, fonds de Fleury, 226 (x.)
6. Vatic. Alexandr., 592 (x. or xi.)
7. Bern., 618 (xi.) ? title.
8. Florent. Laurent., 14, 15 (xi.)
9. Orléans, fonds de Fleury, 232 (xi.)
> Entitled Boetius de fide.
10. Vatic., 567 (xi.)
11. Gotha, 103 and 104 (xi.-xii.)
> Instead of a title there is this note : *ista epistola in aliis libris non invenitur.*
12. St Gall, 768 (xii.)
13. Florent. S. Marco, 167 (xii.)
14. Camb. Univ. Lib., Dd. 6, 6 (xii.)
> At the foot of the page on which iii. ends there follows : *fundamentum catholice fidei a sancto Severino conscriptum.* (See *supra*, p. 140).
15. Rhediger Lib. in Breslau, s. iv. 3 (xii.-xiii.)
16. Vat. Alex., 1975 (xiii.)
17. Vatic., 4250 (xiii.)
18. Florent. Ottobon., 99 (xiii.)
19. Paris, Bibl. Reg. MSS. Lat. 2992 (xiii.)   ? title *eiusdem*.
20. Paris, Bibl. Reg. MSS. Lat. 2376 (xiv.)   ? title *eiusdem*.

D.—MSS. containing only tr. i., ii., iii., and v.

1. Vatic. Alexandr., 208 (x.)
2. St Gall, 134[4] (xi.)
3. Vatic. Alexandr., 1855 (xi.)
4. Valenciennes, 169 (xii.)
5. Florent. s. Croce, 22, 10 (xi.)
6. Vatic., 4251 (xiii.-xiv.)
7. Laon, 123 (xiv.)

E.—MSS. containing only tr. v.

1. Vatic. Urbin., 532 (x.)
2. Vatic. Alexandr., 166 (xi.)

APPENDIX B.

AN INDEX OF PASSAGES IN CHAUCER WHICH SEEM TO HAVE BEEN SUGGESTED BY THE 'DE CONSOLATIONE PHILO-SOPHIÆ.'

THE CANTERBURY TALES.

Prologue.

741-2...................."The word should be germane to the deed."
Cf. Cons., iii. pr. 12, 104 ; tr. 3019-20.[1]

The Knightes Tale.

67-8 ...."Fortune's wheel."
Cf. Cons., ii. pr. 2, 28-9 ; tr. 871-3.

228 * [2]...................."Fortune's changes should be borne with equal mind."
Ib. 44 ; tr. 897.

305-8 ...."Love is above all law."
Cf. Cons., iii. m. 12, 47-8 ; tr. 3063-5.

393-6 *.................."Providence knows what is best for man."
Cf. Cons., iv. pr. 6, 115-7 ; tr. 3991-4.

397-8...................."The desire for riches ; their danger."
Cf. Cons., ii. pr. 5, 92-9 ; tr. 1309-22.
Cf. Cons., ii. m. 5, 30 ; tr. 1351-4.
Cf. Cons., iii. pr. 2, 15-6 ; tr. 1770-2.

404......................"A drunken man cannot find his way home."
Ib. 51 ; tr. 1820.

---

[1] The Chaucer I have used in making this list is the one in the Aldine Series (Bell, 1883) ; the Boethius is Peiper's edition in the Teubner Texts. *Tr.* refers to Chaucer's translation of the De Cons., edited by Dr Morris for the E.E.T.S., 1868.

[2] I have marked with an asterisk all passages which I think are open to question, or such as might be referred to some other source besides Boethius.

408-9....................." False felicity."
                      Ib. 2-5 ; tr. 1753-5.
                      Ib. 50 ; tr. 1817-9.
                      Cf. Cons., iii. m. 8, 1-2 ; tr. 2252-3.
                      Cf. Cons., iii. pr. 11, 115 ; tr. 2829.
445-56..................." Punishment of the innocent."
                      Cf. Cons., i. m. 5, 25-48 ; tr. 526-48.
                      Cf. Cons., iv. pr. 1, 9-18 ; tr. 3096-104.
805-7....................." Destiny the minister of Providence."
                      Cf. Cons., iv. pr. 6, 30-47 : tr. 3869-85 ;
                            esp. 32-4 ; tr. 3870-2.
1088....................." Crœsus."
                      Cf. Cons., ii. pr. 2, 32 ; tr. 877.
1981-3*..............." The changing order of the world ; joy after woe,"
              &c.
                      Cf. Cons., ii. m. 3, 14-5 ; tr. 1001-3.
                      Cf. Cons., ii. m. 8, 1-2 ; tr. 1679-80
2129-35................." The chain of love."
                      Ib. 9-15 ; tr. 1685-9.
2136-41................" The world's changes under the direction of a change-
              less God."
                      Cf. Cons., iv. pr. 6, 21-4 ; tr. 3854-8.
2145-6..................Do.   do.   Ib.   Ib.
2153-7..................Do.   do.   Ib.   Ib.
2147-52................" Every part is derived from a whole."
                      Cf. Cons., iii. pr. 10, 15-7 ; tr. 2471-5.

The Man of Lawes Tale.

29*......................." Merchants compass sea and land for riches."
                      Cf. Cons., ii. m. 5, 14-5 ; tr. 1339-40.
197......................." The Firmament."
                      Cf. Cons., i. m. 5, 1-4 ; tr. 502-4.
                      Cf. Cons., iii. pr. 8, 17 ; tr. 2226.
                      Cf. Cons., iii. pr. 12, 99 ; tr. 3010-4.
                      Cf. Cons., iv. m. 1, 7-8 ; tr. 3138-9.
323......................." Woe the end of human gladness."
                      Cf. Cons., ii. pr. 4, 61-2 ; tr. 1101-2.
382-5..................." Man's ignorance cannot comprehend the working
              of God's Providence."
                      Cf. Cons., iv. pr. 6, 89-92 ; tr. 3951-4.
                      Ib. 117-9 ; tr. 3994-7.
715......................." The ruin of the innocent and the prosperity of the
              wicked."
                      Cf. Cons., i. m. 5, 25-48 ; tr. 526-48.
                      Cf. Cons., iv. pr. 1, 9-18 ; tr. 3096-104.

830-1 ...." The end of sensual pleasures is sorrow."
     Cf. Cons., iii. pr. 7, 1-7 ; tr. 2176-85.

The Prologe of the Wyf of Bathe.

99-101* ...." Vessels of honour and dishonour."
     Cf. Cons., iv. pr. 1, 20, 21 ; tr. 3109-12.

The Wyf of Bathes Tale.

252-68 ...." Gentility tested by noble deeds."
     Cf. Cons., iii. pr. 6, 19-22 ; tr. 2148-55.
     Cf. Cons., iii. m. 6 ; tr. 2169-75.
313-4 .... Do.   do.
     Ib. 6, 7-9 ; tr. 2171-5.
331-2 ...." He that cannot do what he wishes is poor."
     Cf. Cons., iii. pr. 5, 20 ; tr. 2084-6.
347-8..................." Poverty brings to light a man's true friends."
     Cf. Cons., ii. pr. 8, 19-25 ; tr. 1667-78.

The Freres Tale.

185....................." The instruments of God's Providence."
     Cf. Cons., iv. pr. 6, 47-56 ; tr. 3894-907.

The Sompnoures Tale.

260....................." Unity is strength."
     Cf. Cons., iii. pr. 11, 26-9 ; tr. 2694-8.

The Clerkes Tale.

Part V., 26-28 ...." Prosperity is transient ; fortune's changes to be borne with equanimity."
     Cf. Cons., ii. pr. 2, 44 ; tr. 897.
     Cf. Cons., ii. pr. 3, 45 ; tr. 983-4.
Part VI., 217-20 ...." God punishes only to make us better."
     Cf. Cons., iv. pr. 6, 142-4 ; tr. 4032-5.
223....................." God's government is for our good."
     Cf. Cons., iv. pr. 5, 24-5 ; tr. 3791-3.
     Cf. Cons., iv. pr. 6, 190-1 ; tr. 4102-3.

The Marchaundes Tale.

68-70..................." Fortune's gifts."
     Cf. Cons., ii. pr. 2, 16 ; tr. 854.
     Cons., ii. pr. 5, *passim ;* tr. 1170-322.

540......................" The familiar foe."
  Cf. Cons., iii. pr. 5, 40 ; tr. 2114.
722......................" The instruments of Providence."
  See above, Frére's Tale, 185.
  Cf. Cons., iv. pr. 6, 47-50 ; tr. 3894-7.
777-8....................." The doctrine of Epicurus."
  Cf. Cons., iii. pr. 2, 46-7 ; tr. 1813-4.
818-20 ...." The wiles of the monster, Fortune."
  Cf. Cons., ii. pr. 1, 6-9 ; tr. 739-43.

The Squyeres Tale.

Part I., 250-3 ...." Things whose causes are hidden make men wonder."
  Cf. Cons., iv. m. 5, 9-22 ; tr. 3803-22.
Part II., 262-3......." All things seek their kind with joy."
  Cf. Cons., iii. m. 2, 34-5 ; tr. 1882-4.
265-70..................." The caged bird."
  Ib. 17-26 ; tr. 1867-76.

The Frankeleynes Tale.

137-9....................." God the governor of all things."
  Cf. Cons., i. m. 5, 25 ; tr. 526.
  Cf. Cons., iii. m. 9, 1 ; tr. 2414-6.
151......................." Mankind a fair part of God's work."
  Cf. Cons., i. m. 5, 44 ; tr. 543-4.
158......................" All is for the best."
  Cf. Cons., iv. pr. 6, *passim*, esp. 150 ;
  tr. 4042-5.
303....... ...." The God that gives to plants and trees their proper
  times and seasons."
  Cf. Cons., i. m. 6; esp. 16, 17 ; tr. 623-4.

The Secounde Nonnes Tale.

114....................." The Firmament."
  Cf. Cons., i. m. 5, 3 ; tr. 504.
  Cf. Cons., iii. pr. 8, 17 ; tr. 2226.
  Cf. Cons., iv. m. 1, 7, 8 ; tr. 3138-9.

The Prologe of the Chanounes Yeman.

405......................" Human impotency."
  Cf. Cons., iii. pr. 9, 62-3 ; tr. 2359-61.

The Tale of Melibeus.

P. 152*............." Avarice is insatiable."
  Cf. Cons., ii. m. 2, 17-8 ; tr. 913-5.

P. 163 ...."Good the contrary of evil."

                    Cf. Cons., iv. pr. 2, 6 ; tr. 3174.

P. 173 ...."Fortune the nurse."

                    Cf. Cons., ii. pr. 2, 10 ; tr. 845.

The Monkes Tale.

105-20 ...."The labours of Hercules."

                    Cf. Cons., iv. m. 7, 13-28 ; tr. 4257-84.

149-52* ...."The uncertainty of Fortune, against which self-knowledge is the only safeguard."

                    Cf. Cons., ii. pr. 4, 70-2 ; tr. 1115-7.

251-5 ...."Misfortune turns friends to foes."

                    Cf. Cons., iii. pr. 5, 37-8 ; tr. 2111-3.

357 ...."The gall in Fortune's honey."

                    Cf. Cons., ii. pr. 4, 61-2 ; tr. 1102.

407-8 ...."Fortune's wheel and capriciousness."

                    Cf. Cons., ii. pr. 1, 40-1 ; tr. 790.

                    Cf. Cons., ii. pr. 2, 28-9 ; tr. 871-3.

455-6* ...."Fortune the cause of calamity."

                    Cf. Cons., ii. pr. 1, 4 ; tr. 734-5.

473-500 ...."Nero."

                    Cf. Cons., ii. m. 6 ; tr. 1458-79 ; esp. 1-7 ; tr. 1458-67.

                    Cf. Cons., iii. m. 4, 1-2 ; tr. 2048-50.

733-4 ...."Fortune's inconstancy."

                    Cf. Cons., ii. pr. 1, 37 ; tr. 782.

736-41 ...."Crœsus rescued by rain."

                    Cf. Cons., ii. pr. 2, 32-4 ; tr. 877-81.

770-3 ...."A definition of tragedy."

                    Ib. 36-8 ; tr. 884-6.

774-6 ...."Fortune covers her face."

                    Cf. Cons., ii. pr. 1, 31-2 ; tr. 773-4.

The Nonne Prest his Tale.

180 ...."Fortune the common mistress of us all."

                    Cf. Cons., ii. pr. 2, 44 ; tr. 897.

414 ...."God's foreknowledge implies necessity."

                    Cf. Cons., v. pr. 3, 7 ; tr. 4445.

423-30 ...."God's foreknowledge and man's freewill."

                    Cf. Cons., v. pr. 3, 4, and 6, *passim*, esp. pr. 3, 4-10 ; tr. 4440-9 ; pr. 3, 26-30 ; tr. 4474-9 ; pr. 4, 25-6 ; tr. 4693-4 ; pr. 4, 48-9 ; tr. 4724-5 ; pr. 6, 99-122 ; tr. 5116-43 ; pr. 6, 129-32 ; tr. 5156-9.

The Maunciples Tale.

56-8......................" Nature's law is irrefragable."
Cf. Cons., iii. m. 2, 3-4 ; tr. 1855-6.
59-70....................." The caged bird."
Ib. 17-26 ; tr. 1867-76.

The Persones Tale.

P. 275* ...." The shadow is not the substance."
Cf. Cons., v. pr. 4, 31-2 ; tr. 4701-2.
P. 302..................." The folly of trusting to Fortune's gifts."
Cf. Cons., ii. m. 3, 15-6 ; tr. 1003-4.
P. 302..................." The danger of sensual pleasures."
Cf. Cons., iii. pr. 7, 3-5 ; tr. 2178-81.

THE ASSEMBLY OF FOULES.

380-1....................." The harmonious concord of the elements."
Cf. Cons., iii. pr. 11, 71-3 ; tr. 2760-3.
599-60..................." Owls are blind by day, but see at night."
Cf. Cons., iv. pr. 4, 91 ; tr. 3655-6.

TROYLUS AND CRYSEYDE.

Book I.

St. 105, 730..........." Lethargy."
Cf. Cons., i. pr. 2, 11 ; tr. 140.
Ib. 731................."'Όνος λύρας."
Cf. Cons., i. pr. 4, 2 ; tr. 247.
St. 113 ...." Tityus and the vultures."
Cf. Cons., iii. m. 12, 38-9 ; tr. 3053-4.
St. 120, 837..........." Fortune my foe."
Cf. Cons., i. pr. 4, 6 ; tr. 254.
Ib. 838-40............." Fortune's wheel."
Cf. Cons., ii. pr. 1, 56-7 ; tr. 816.
Cf. Cons., ii. pr. 2, 28-9 ; tr. 871-3.
St. 121, 843-4........" All are liable to Fortune's changes."
Ib. 44-5 ; tr. 847.
Ib. 846-7..............." Adversity, like prosperity, is transient."
Cf. Cons., ii. pr. 3, 39-41 ; tr. 975-8.
St. 122, 848-9........" Fortune's changing wheel."
Cf. Cons., ii. pr. 1, 57-8 ; tr. 817-8.
Ib. 850-4............." Her very mutability gives promise of better things.
Cf. Cons., ii. pr. 2, 42-3 ; tr. 895-6.

266 BOETHIUS.

Book II.

Proem ; st. 6, 42...."Each country has its own laws."

Cf. Cons., ii. pr. 7, 36-7 ; tr. 1541-3.

St. 76, 526-8 ...."God shapes our ends."

Cf. Cons., iv. pr. 6, 115-7 ; tr. 3991-4.

St. 110, 766-7 ...."Wind dispels clouds."

Cf. Cons., i. m. 3, 7-8 ; tr. 157-8.

Book III.

Proem ; st. 2........."The power of Love."

Cf. Cons., ii. m. 8 ; esp. 13-5 ; tr. 1688-90.

St. 47, 324* ...."God the Governor."

Cf. Cons., iii. m. 9, 1 ; tr. 2414-5.

St. 82, 568-71........"Providence controls the stars ; fortune and fate are its ministers."

Cf. Cons., iv. pr. 6, 48-57, esp. 50, 57 ; tr. 3894-906.

St. 110, 764-6........"The bitterness of worldly joys."

Cf. Cons., ii. pr. 4, 61-2 ; tr. 1101-2.

Ib. 767-70............."The condition of human happiness."

Ib. 39-41 ; tr. 1066-81.

Ib. 64-6 ; tr. 1105-9.

St. 111-112... ...."Its brittleness."

Ib. 79-86 ; tr. 1127-40.

St. 113, 786*........."No happiness in this world."

Ib. 94 ; tr. 1152-3.

St. 174, 1212........."The bond of love."

Cf. Cons., ii. m. 8, 13-5 ; tr. 1688-9.

St. 226, 1576-9......."The pain of past happiness."

Cf. Cons., ii. pr. 4, 4-6 ; tr. 1012-4.

St. 243-6..............."The bond of love."

Cf. Cons., ii. m. 8 ; tr. 1679-99.

St. 254................."Fortune's cruel sport."

Cf. Cons., ii. m. 1 ; esp. 4-6 ; tr. 825-9.

Ib........................"Her rolling wheel."

Cf. Cons., ii. pr. 2, 28-9 ; tr. 871-3.

Book IV.

St. 52, 363-4........."No man has a right in fortune's gifts ; they are 'in commune.'"

Ib. 6 ; tr. 840-1.

Ib. 44 ; tr. 897.

St. 65, 454-5........."Present pain is the keener for past happiness."

Cf. Cons., ii. pr. 4, 4-6 ; tr. 1012-4.

St. 68, 475-6..........." Death the desired deliverer."

                                Cf. Cons., i. m. 1, 13-4 ; tr. 16-7.

St. 116, 807-8........." The wretchedness of mortal bliss."

                                Cf. Cons., ii. pr. 4, 64-6 ; tr. 1105-9.

St. 133, 930....... ....." Necessity and Freewill."

                                Cf. Cons., v. pr. 2, 26-8 ; tr. 4420-3.

St. 150..............." Necessity and Freewill."

                                Cf. Cons., v. pr. 3, 1-53 ; tr. 4437-513.

St. 223, 1559-60....." How to command Fortune."

                                Cf. Cons., ii. pr. 4, 71-2 ; tr. 1116-7.

Book V.

St. 40, 278 .... " Phœbus' rosy car."

                                Cf. Cons., ii. m. 3, 1 ; tr. 990.

St. 109, 762..........." Felicity is sufficiency."

                                Cf. Cons., iii. pr. 2, 5-6 ; tr. 1756-8.

St. 222, 1554-6*....." Fortune controlled by Providence."

                                Cf. Cons., iv. pr. 6, 21-4 ; tr. 3854-8.

St. 260, 1823-6......." A soul's journey to the seventh sphere (the highest point of heaven)."

                                Cf. Cons., iv. m. 1, 16-8 ; tr. 3150-3.

THE BOKE OF THE DUCHESSE.

588....................." Tityus."

                                Cf. Cons., iii. m. 12, 39 ; tr. 3053.

623....................." Fortune the ' debonaire.' "

                                Cf. Cons., ii. pr. 8, 9 ; tr. 1649.

627....................." Fortune the monster."

                                Cf. Cons., ii. pr. 1, 6 ; tr. 739.

634 and 642..........." Her capriciousness and her rolling wheel."

                                Cf. Cons., ii. pr. 2, 28-9 ; tr. 871-2.

708....................." Tantalus."

                                Cf. Cons., iii. m. 12, 36-7 ; tr. 3052.

778....................." The mind compared to a clean parchment."

                                Cf. Cons., v. m. 4, 6-9 ; tr. 4837-9.

1055-6 ...." Alcibiades."

                                Cf. Cons., iii. pr. 8, 24 ; tr. 2237.

THE HOUSE OF FAME.

Book II.

28........................" The thunderbolt."

                                Cf. Cons., i. m. 4, 9-10 ; tr. 236-7.

221-48 .... " The instinct of self-preservation in nature."
                              Cf. Cons., iii. pr. 11, *passim*, esp. 69-
                              81 ; tr. 2756-74.

Book III.

278-85 ...." Nature's variable stature."
                              Cf. Cons., i. pr. 1, 7-11 ; tr. 37-41.
455-9 .... " Fortune's unfair distribution of rewards."
                              Cf. Cons., i. pr. 5, 34 ; tr. 598-9.
830 .... " The house of Dædalus."
                              Cf. Cons., iii. pr. 12, 77 ; tr. 2981.

THE LEGENDE OF GOODE WOMEN.

Philomene.

343-5 .... " The world's prototype."
                              Cf. Cons., iii. m. 9, 7-8 ; tr. 2422-4.

BALLADE DE VISAGE SAUNS PEYNTURE.[1]

1-4 .... " Fortune's tricks."
                              Cf. Cons., ii. m. 1, 3-4 ; tr. 823-6.
10-12 .... " Fortune teaches us to distinguish between friend
                              and foe."
                              Cf. Cons., ii. pr. 8, 19-20 ; tr. 1667-8.
13 .... " Self-mastery a safeguard against Fortune."
                              Cf. Cons., ii. pr. 4, 71-2 ; tr. 1116-7.
17 .... " Socrates."
                              Cf. Cons., i. pr. 3, 18 and 29 ; tr. 186
                              and 206.
25-48 .... " Fortune's reply to her accuser."
                              For the general idea, cf. Cons., ii. pr. 2.
25-28 .... " To command one's self is to command Fortune."
                              Cf. Cons., ii. pr. 4, 71-2 ; tr. 1116-7.
29-30 .... " Thanks are owing to Fortune for her loan of goods."
                              Cf. Cons., ii. pr. 2, 13-4 ; tr. 850.
31 .... " Her changefulness gives hope of better things."
                              Ib. 41-2 ; tr. 895-6.
33-4 .... " She teaches to distinguish friend from foe."
                              Cf. Cons., ii. pr. 8, 20-5 ; tr. 1668-78.

---

[1] The title, as given by Morris and the old editions, is " Ballade de
Vilage." The mistake arose from confusing *f* with *l*. (See Skeat's ' Minor
Poems of Chaucer,' p. 374.)

38......................."The anchor [of hope] still holds."
                    Cf. Cons., ii. pr. 4, 30-1 ; tr. 1050-1.
42-4...................."Shall the slave dictate to the mistress?"
                    Cf. Cons., ii. p. 1, 49-50 and 55 ; tr.
                        802-5 and 813-5.
45 ...."Fortune's common realm."
                    Cf. Cons., ii. pr. 2, 44 ; tr. 897.
46......................."Fortune's wheel."
                    Cf. Cons., ii. pr. 1, 56-7 ; tr. 815-7, and
                        pr. 2, 28-9 ; tr. 871-2.
50-2...................."Fortune's friends."
                    Cf. Cons., ii. pr. 8, 19-22 ; tr. 1667
                        78.
57-64...................."Fortune's reply continued."
                    Cf. Cons., ii. pr. 2, 10-27 ; tr. 845-69.
66-7 ...."Providence."
                    Cf. Cons., iv. pr. 6, 30-2 ; tr. 3868-71.
68......................."Men addressed as beasts."
                    Cf. Cons., iii. pr. 3, 1 ; tr. 1888.
71 ...."The end of Fortune."
                    Cf. Cons., ii. pr. 3, 45-6 ; tr. 984-5.

BALLADE SENT TO KING RICHARD.

For the general idea of this poem, " Lack of steadfastness," cf. Cons.,
    ii. m. 8. 1-4 ; tr. 1679-81 ; ib. 13-21 ; tr. 1688-704 ; ib. 28-30 ; tr.
    1707-8.

GOOD COUNSEIL OF CHAUCER.

2......................"Be content with little."
                    Cf. Cons., ii. pr. 5, 40-2 ; tr. 1231-3.
3. ...."Avarice is ever odious."
                    Cf. Cons., ii. pr. 5, 9-10 ; tr. 1182-3.
Ib ...."Ambition is dangerous."
                    Cf. Cons., iii. pr. 8, 8-9 ; tr. 2213-5.
7........................."Truth the great criterion."
                    Cf. Cons., iii. m. 11, 7-8 ; tr. 2840-2 ;
                        ib. 11-4 ; tr. 2860-8.
......................"Calmness commended."[1]
                    Cf. Cons., ii. pr. 4, 35 ; tr. 1060.

_____

[1] Morris reads "peyne the not"; Skeat, "tempest the not"; and
this last suits the passage in Boece, "tempest nat the thus."

9........................." The whirling wheel."
> Cf. Cons., ii. pr. 2, 28-9 ; tr. 871-2, &c.

15........................." Contentment commended."
> Cf. Cons., ii. pr. 1, 47 ; tr. 800-1.

17........................." The heavenly home."
> Cf. Cons., i. pr. 5, 9 and 11 ; tr. 561-2 and 565-6.
>
> Cf. Cons., iii. pr. 12, 27 ; tr. 2911.
>
> Cf. Cons., iv. pr. 1, 32 and 35 ; tr. 3128 and 3132.
>
> Cf. Cons., iv. m. 1, 25 ; tr. 3159 and 3132.
>
> Cf. Cons., v. pr. 1, 9 ; tr. 4305.

18........................." Man addressed as a beast."
> Cf. Cons., iii. pr. 3, 1 ; tr. 1888.
>
> Cf. Cons., iv. pr. 3, 66 ; tr. 3478.
>
> Cf. Cons., iv. m. 3, *passim*.
>
> Cf. Cons., iv. pr. 4, 3 ; tr. 3519.

19........................." The heavenly home."
> See above on l. 17.

Ib........................." Look up." [1]
> Cf. Cons., v. m. 5, 10-3 ; tr. 4968-72.

A BALLADE (p. 296).

For the general idea, and the definition of gentility, cf. Cons., iii. pr. 6, 20-7 ; tr. 2150-63 ; and m. 6, 1-2 and 6-9 ; tr. 2164-6 and 2170-5.

AETAS PRIMA.

For the general idea, and the former age, cf. Cons., ii. m. 5.

---

[1] " Loke up on hye and thonke God of alle."—Morris.
" Know thy contree, lok up, thank God of al."—Skeat.

ADDENDUM to p. 218.

Since chapter vi. passed through the press, Professor Skeat has announced his discovery that the originals of the notes and glosses in Chaucer's translation are to be found in the Cambridge MS., Ii. 3, 21. (See 'The Athenæum' of Oct. 24, 1891.

INDEX.